Pragmatism

PRAGMATISM

An Open Question

Hilary Putnam

BLACKWELL
Oxford UK & Cambridge USA

Copyright © Hilary Putnam 1995

The right of Hilary Putnam to be identified as author of this work has been asserted in accordance with the Copyright, Designs and Patents Act 1988.

The bibliography is published by permission of Rowohlt Taschenbuch Verlag GmbH,
Reinbek bei Hamburg.

Originally published in Italian as *Il Pragmatismo: Una Questione Aperta.*
Copyright © 1992, Gius, Laterza & Figli Spa, Roma-Bari.

First published in English 1995
Reprinted 1995, 1996 (twice), 1999, 2000

Transferred to digital print 2006

Blackwell Publishers Inc
350 Main Street
Malden, Massachusetts 02148, USA

Blackwell Publishers Ltd
108 Cowley Road
Oxford OX4 1JF, UK

Library of Congress Cataloging in Publication Data
Putnam, Hilary
Pragmatism : an open question / Hilary Putnam.
    p.   cm.
Includes bibliographical references and index.
ISBN 0–631–19342–1 (alk. paper) — ISBN 0–631–19343–X (pbk)
1. Pragmatism. 2. James Williams, 1842–1910. 3. Wittgenstein, Ludwig, 1889–1951. I. Title.
B832.P94   1995
144'.3—dc20   94–21503
                                                                CIP

British Library Cataloguing in Publication Data
A CIP catalogue record for this book is available from the British Library

Typeset in 11 ½ on 13 ½ pt Bembo
by CentraCet Limited, Cambridge
Printed and bound in Great Britain by Marston Book Services Limited, Oxford

This book is printed on acid-free paper

To James Conant

Contents

Hilary Putnam

Hilary Putnam was born in Chicago in 1926. He took his B.A. in the University of Pennsylvania in 1948 and his Ph.D. at UCLA under the supervision of Hans Reichenbach in 1951. His doctoral topic was on the concept of probability. (This has recently been published under the title *The Meaning of the Concept of Probability in Application to Finite Sequences: with an Introduction Some Years Later*, by Garland, 1990.) After teaching in Northwestern University and in the Mathematics and Philosophy departments at Princeton, he joined the Faculty of MIT as Professor of the Philosophy of Science in 1961.

In the late 1950s he, together with Martin Davies and Julia Robinson, found the solution of the problem of the decidability of exponential diophantine equations and so provided the key to the solution of the tenth member of the list of major outstanding mathematical problems bequeathed to twentieth-century mathematics by David Hilbert.

In 1965 he moved to Harvard University as Professor of Philosophy and in 1976 was appointed Walter Beverley Pearson Professor of Mathematical Logic.

In the early 1960s he published a sequence of papers beginning with the now classic "Minds and Machines", which launched the "functionalist" account of mental life and which did so much to clarify the relationship between theories of computation, computability and the "mind–body" problem. In the 1970s he made outstanding contributions to the philosophy of language and the philosophy of natural science and mathematics; his work on the philosophy of space and time and the philosophy of geometry being particularly well known. In cooperation with the physicist David Finkelstein, he began an investigation into the foundations of quantum theory, which produced a series of papers on quantum logic, an investigation which is still continuing.

In 1976 he was elected President of the American Philosophical Association and in 1980 President of the Association of Symbolic Logic. In 1986 he gave the Carus lectures, which were published as *The Many Faces of Realism* in 1987 (Open Court); and in 1990 he gave the Gifford lectures in St Andrews, which were published as *Renewing Philosophy* (Harvard University Press, 1992).

Hilary Putnam is married to the American moral philosopher Ruth Anna Putnam, who teaches at Wellesley College, Massachusetts.

Preface

In 1991, Pino Donghi, Enrico Mistretta and Lorena Preta raised the idea of my giving a series of lectures in Rome "on my current philosophical interests." I once again express my gratitude to them for this opportunity. As a result of their suggestion, in March 1992 I gave these three lectures in the distinguished series "Lezione italiane" under the sponsorship of the Sigma Tau Foundation and the Laterza publishing house, at the Università degli Studi di Roma "La Sapienza." Apart from a few changes in the first one, the present volume contains the text of those lectures as they were delivered.

As the title indicates, I chose to talk about Pragmatism – not Pragmatism as a movement that had its day at the end of the nineteenth and the beginning of the twentieth century, but as a way of thinking that I find of lasting importance, and an option (or at least an "open question") that should figure in present-day philosophical thought. And since the invitation was to talk about "my current interests," I did not hesitate to talk about the ways in which I see the later philosophy of Wittgenstein as also paralleling certain themes in Pragmatism.

In a short series of lectures, there was no question of my attempting an exhaustive account of Pragmatism, or even of constructing a detailed argument for the correctness of those Pragmatist positions that I find sympathetic, although I do try to correct misunderstandings of Pragmatism and to reply to a number of likely objections. I have not chosen to focus on James's theory of truth, or to see Peirce or James or Dewey primarily as participants in a debate about realism and antirealism. Rather, in the present lectures I stress the *pluralism* and the thoroughgoing *holism* which are ubiquitous in Pragmatist writing. If the vision of fact, theory, value and interpretation as interpenetrating undermines a certain sort of metaphysical realism, it equally, I believe, undermines fashionable versions of antirealism and "postmodernism." In this short volume I try to articulate that vision, and develop its significance.

Cambridge, Massachusetts
Harvard University, 1994

Introductory Remarks

Today we tend to take the ideas of tolerance and pluralism for granted. If we are aware that there was diversity of views and the clash of different opinions in ancient Athens, for example, or in the late Roman empire, we are likely to regard that activity as a sign of vitality in those societies. Few people realize that that is not how those societies themselves saw the matter. Classical thinkers saw diversity of opinions as a sign of decay and heresy; only since the Enlightenment have we been able to see it as a positive good. One author[1] has suggested that it is only when society came to be held together "through an alliance of enlightened self interest, rather than through shared moral and religious beliefs" that "the flourishing of diversity and pluralism, which in the past have existed only as a by-product and symptom of political decline, could be embraced for the first time as a form of social health." While this author exaggerates – modern liberal states are still held together by sentiment and tradition as well as by self interest, enlightened or not so enlightened – and while he fails to see that the belief in tolerance is itself a "shared moral belief", and a most important one, it is true that modern societies are not held together by a single shared comprehensive world view. They are not held together by any one religion, and if there are still shared moral beliefs, there are no *unchallenged* moral beliefs. Moreover, except for a minority of reactionaries, we do not wish that our societies should be held together by unquestioned systems of moral and religious belief. We value our freedom to choose our own "destinies" (to use a term suggested by Agnes Heller[2]), where that freedom is understood as not merely the freedom to choose a trade or profession, but also as the freedom to decide for oneself regarding values, goals, concrete norms, and even, to a certain extent, mores.

What we call the Enlightenment was in large part an intellectual movement devoted to providing a rationale for this kind of "open society"; it was not only a political and historical rationale, but also an epistemological rationale, one which included "arguments about the uncertainty of our moral and religious knowledge."[3] And the problems generated by the Englightenment are still our problems; we value the tolerance and pluralism, but we are troubled by the epistemological scepticism that came with that tolerance and pluralism.

I remind you of all this, because the issues that I will be discussing are not just theoretical issues. It is an open question whether an enlightened society can avoid a corrosive moral scepticism without tumbling back into moral authoritarianism. And it is precisely this question that has led me, in recent years, back to pragmatism – to the writings of Peirce, and James and Dewey, and also to the writings of Wittgenstein, whose work, I shall argue in these lectures, bears affinities to American Pragmatism even if he was not willing to be classed as a "pragmatist".

In the first of the lectures that follow, I try to explain

the importance of the thought of William James, focussing in particular on the way in which fact and value are seen as inseparable by James, but also setting the stage for the discussion of the inseparability of fact and theory and fact and interpretation in the lectures which follow. In the second lecture, I try to situate the later philosophy of Wittgenstein not only with respect to pragmatism, but also with respect to the history of philosophy, and in the third and final lecture I try to bring the legacy of Peirce, James, Dewey, and Wittgenstein to bear on some of our contemporary philosophical debates. In particular, I hope to convince you that pragmatism offers something far better than the unpalatable alternatives which too often seem to be the only possibilities today, both philosophically and politically.

Notes

1 Arthur M. Melzer. See his "Tolerance 101," in *The New Republic*, June 1991.
2 See her *A Philosophy of Morals* (Oxford: Basil Blackwell, 1990).
3 Melzer, pp. 11–12.

1

The Permanence of William James

William James is a figure who simply won't go away. Not only has he never been forgotten, but the reactions to his work after his death, both the favorable and the unfavorable, have been surprisingly passionate. In his *History of Western Philosophy*, Bertrand Russell holds James's views on truth up to ridicule. Yet a great contemporary of Russell's wrote, "The view that seems to me to reconcile the materialistic tendencies of psychology with the anti-materialistic tendency of physics is the view of . . . the American new realists . . . Their views . . . . are in large measure derived from William James, and before going further it will be well to consider the revolutionary doctrine which he advanced. I believe this doctrine contains important new truth, and what I shall have to say will be in considerable measure inspired by it."[1]

Who was this contemporary? It was none other than Russell himself! The Russell of *The Analysis of Mind*. (In fairness to Russell, there is no contradiction here; Russell despised James's views on truth, of which he presents a mere caricature, but admired James's "neutral monism" – which was Russell's term for what James himself called "radical empiricism." In fact, I. B. Cohen recently told me that when Russell lectured at Harvard in 1936, "there were two heros in his lectures – Plato and James".) Coming closer to our own time, in 1983, Martin Gardner, the well-known writer of columns of mathematical puzzles for *Scientific American* and debunker of telepathy and other things that he regards as fraudulent science, devoted a chapter of a book about his own philosophical convictions[2] to criticizing James's account of truth. (Gardner, I hasten to add, does not regard James as a fraud, but he does think that "There was a blindness on James's part . . . to the kind of confusion that is inevitable when a philosopher takes a word with a commonly understood meaning and gives it a new and novel meaning. Pragmatists believed, of course, that great benefits would flow from redefining truth as the meeting of tests for truth [sic]. but the actual results were decades of bewildering debate in which they wasted incredible amounts of time."[3] In the same year (1983) Jacques Barzun published his lovely volume, *A Stroll with William James*, in appreciation of "the originality and force of mind by which James met and subdued some of the old Sphinxes who challenge the earthly traveler, as always on pain of death."[4]

My purpose in adding to this cloud of praise and criticism that swirls around the figure of William James is not simply homage to a predecessor. I believe that James was a powerful thinker, as powerful as any in the last century, and that his way of philosophizing contains possibilities which have been too long neglected, that it points to ways out of old philosophical "binds" that continue to afflict us. In short, I believe that it is high time we paid attention to Pragmatism, the movement of which James was arguably the greatest exponent.

I hasten to add – to your relief, I am sure – that this

lecture will not pretend to be the detailed and penetrating study that we need. It is rather an advertisement for that project, a presentation of the *prima facie* case for thinking that the project is worthwhile.

I can begin by indicating one of the reasons that James's philosophy evokes such contradictory responses. One of the chief characteristics of James's philosophy is its *holism*: there is an obvious if implicit rejection of many familiar dualisms: fact, value, and theory are all seen by James[5] as interpenetrating and interdependent. (In the third lecture, I shall also defend the idea that interpretation (of meanings, and of forms of life) and knowledge of facts similarly interpenetrate, along lines that I believe James would approve.) Another characteristic of that philosophy – one which confused at least one of James's principal followers[6] – is a strong strain of what philosophers used to call *direct realism*, that is, the doctrine that perception is (normally) of objects and events "out there", and not of private "sense data". Holism and direct realism can seem inconsistent: that is how they seemed to the Oxford philosopher F. C. S. Schiller, the follower I mentioned, to whom the realism represented backsliding of some sort on James's part, and that is how they seemed to Bertrand Russell, to whom they represented two distinct moments in James's thought, the first misguided and the second full of insight. It is my conviction, and that of Ruth Anna Putnam, who is collaborating with me on a study of James's philosophy, that far from being inconsistent these two aspects of James's philosophy are interdependent; each presupposes the other, and each is necessary for the proper interpretation of the other. But I shall not try to substantiate this interpretative claim in detail; instead, I shall just try to give you some idea of what each of them comes to.

Truth

The passage which is most often plucked out of context and used as a stick with which to beat James is the following: "The 'true' is only the expedient in the way of our thinking . . . in the long run and on the whole of course." That is verbatim how Russell quotes it. As his critics read this, what James is saying is that if the consequences of believing that *p* are good for humanity,[7] then *p* is true. It is thus that Russell can write, "I find great intellectual difficulties in this doctrine. It assumes that a belief is 'true' when its effects are good."[8] But this is not what James means; indeed, it is not even what James *says*. What he actually wrote is:

> *"The true,"* to put it very briefly, is only the expedient in the way of our thinking, just as *"the right"* is only the expedient in the way of our behaving. Expedient in almost any fashion; and expedient in the long run and on the whole of course, for what meets expediently all the experience in sight won't necessarily meet all further experiences equally satisfactorily. Experience, as we know, has ways of *boiling over*, and making us correct our present formulas.[9]

I am not going to try your patience with close textual analysis – I shall, henceforth, just say dogmatically what I think James intends, without marshalling proof texts – but I cannot resist pointing out how Russell's misreading of James resembles a common misreading of an equally famous passage of Wittgenstein's. Wittgenstein wrote, "For a *large* class of cases – though not for all – in which we employ the word 'meaning' it can be defined thus: the meaning of a word is its use in the language."[10] Here many commentators simply ignore "though not for all", and also substitute their own notion of what "use" is for Wittgenstein's, and end up saying that Wittgenstein proposed the "theory" that "meaning is use" – at which point all possibility of understanding what Wittgenstein is actually saying vanishes! In the same way, Russell ignores "to put it very briefly" and "in *almost* any fashion" – obvious indications that what we have is a thematic statement, and not an attempt to formulate a definition of "true" – and also substitutes his own notion of what "expediency" is for James's, and ends up saying that James proposed the theory that "true" means "has good effects" – at which point all possibility of understanding what James is actually saying vanishes!

The fact is James's philosophy cannot be put in a nutshell any more than Wittgenstein's. But what follows thematic statements like the one just quoted[11] in James's text, and in his other writings, are discussions of major *types* of statements, for example, statements about Memorial Hall and other perceivable objects, statements about more abstract things like the elasticity of the clock spring, statements in contemporary physical theories, mathematical statements, ethical statements, and religious statements. It emerges that different types of statements correspond to different *types* of "expediency"; there is no suggestion that an arbitrary statement is true if it is expedient in any way at all (even "in the long run"). For example, the view often attributed to James – that a statement is true if it will make people subjectively *happy* to believe it – is explicitly *rejected* by him.[12] In the case of paradigm "factual" statements, including scientific ones, a sort of expediency that James repeatedly mentions is usefulness for prediction,[13] while other desiderata – conservation of past doctrine;[14] simplicity,[15] and coherence ("what fits every part of life best and combines with the collectivity of experience's demands, nothing being omitted"[16], p. 44) – are said to apply to statements of all types. Quine's claim[17] that success in satisfying these desiderata simultaneously is a matter of trade-offs rather than formal rules is also a Jamesian idea.[18]

A second criticism of James – one sometimes made by admirers of James, like Morton White, as well as by critics like Martin Gardner – is that James is really talking about *confirmation* and not about truth. James is giving us an account of *confirmation*, these critics say, and he mistakenly believes that he is giving us an account of truth. The critics also claim that the problem of giving us a satisfactory account of truth was solved in this century, by the work of the great logician Alfred Tarski. I myself believe[19] that Tarski's great technical contribution notwithstanding, his work does *nothing* to explicate the notion of truth, but that is not my topic here. However James is *not* guilty of confounding confirmation and truth,[20] although he certainly believes there is a close connection.

The connection exists for the following reasons: To say that truth is "correspondence to reality" is not false but *empty*, as long as nothing is said about what the "correspondence" is. If the "correspondence" is supposed to be utterly independent of the ways in which we confirm the assertions we make (so that it is conceived to be possible that what is true is utterly *different* from what we are warranted in *taking to be true*, not just in some cases but in all cases), then the "correspondence" is an occult one, and our supposed grasp of it is also occult. Truth, James believes, must be such that we can say how it is possible for us to grasp what it is. And like Peirce, he frequently identifies truth with the "final opinion", that is, not with what is presently confirmed, but with what is "fated" to be confirmed, if inquiry is continued long enough, and in a responsible and fallibilistic spirit. Truth, James writes in one place is "the fate of thought". And (in the same place), "The only objective criterion of reality is coerciveness, in the long run, over thought."[21]

This is, of course, a very problematical position, although different elements of it continue to be reinvented and hotly discussed today, by philosophers some of whom never mention James. Let me just point out that these issues – the relationship of truth, warranted assertibility, permanent credibility, what, if anything, inquiry must converge to if conducted in the right way, etc. – figure today in books and papers by the Putnams, Michael Dummett, Nelson Goodman, Richard Rorty and Bernard Williams, who hold different and sometimes even opposed positions on these issues, but all of whom take very seriously just the point that James insisted on, that our grasp of the notion of truth must not be represented as simply a mystery mental act by which we relate ourselves to a relation called "correspondence" totally independent of the practices by which we *decide* what is and is not true.

To be sure, rejection of that sort of metaphysical realism does not require us to follow the pragmatists in identifying the true with what is (or what would be) "verified" in the long run. Unlike the pragmatists, I do not believe that truth can be *defined* in terms of verification. (Readers who are interested in my own most recent account of the concept of truth will find it presented in my Dewey Lectures, "Sense, Nonsense, and the Senses; An Inquiry Into the Powers of the Human Mind"[22].) Yet I do agree with the pragmatists that truth and verification are not simply independent and unrelated notions. Knowing, for example, what it is to verify that there is a chair in front of me involves knowing what chairs look like, what we use them for, and what it is like to sit on one. But someone who lacked these abilities – for what this sort of knowledge comes to is just the possession of a set of practical abilities – would not just lack the ability to *confirm* the claim "There is a chair in front of me"; such a person would lack the very concept of a chair, and hence would lack the ability to understand what it is for "There is a chair in front of me" to be *true*.

I do not mean to suggest that for *every* statement it is the case that to understand it requires knowing how to confirm it. Yet even if we take a statement we do not at all know how to confirm (say, "Intelligent extraterrestrial life does not exist"), the fact is that the concepts which it employs are concepts which figure in other and simpler statements which we do know how to verify. Our ability to understand such an 'unverifiable" statement is not a *free standing* ability. Understanding what truth is in any given case and understanding what confirmation is are interwoven abilities; and this is something that the pragmatists were among the first to see, even if (like any philosopher who first formulates an insight) they formulated their idea too simply. James's "theory of truth" may have been wrong, but he knew perfectly well the difference between truth and confirmation, and he was not simply confusing the two. What he believed was that, since our claims get their substance from the roles they play in our lives, an account of truth will gain its substance from the accompanying account of how to get to truth. As he himself puts it, "If I tell you how to get to the railroad station, don't I implicitly introduce you to the *what*, to the being and nature of that edifice?"[23]

Holism

As I have explained it so far, James's position can sound like positivism, and indeed the first misunderstanding of Pragmatism that James discusses in "The Pragmatist Account of Truth and its Misunderstanders"[24] is that "Pragmatism is only a re-editing of positivism".[25] James's reply is to disassociate himself from the phenomenalism of contemporary (Machian) positivism. Pragmatism does not assert that knowledge is confined to the succession of our *sensations*. But our present-day Neopositivists (I hope Van Quine will not object if I classify him as such) are no more phenomenalistic than James was, and I have already said that, at least in the case of scientific statements, James and Quine both see warranted assertibility as a matter of "trade-offs" between very similar desiderata – prediction, conservation of old doctrine, simplicity and overall coherence. For this very reason, it is necessary to distinguish James's position from Neopositivism if we are to make out its present-day interest.

The difference has to do with the rejection of familiar dualisms – fact and value, fact and theory, fact and interpretation – that I mentioned at the outset of this talk. That rejection is, by the way, the first pragmatist theme that I was to be exposed to in my own undergraduate education. That education took place at the University of Pennsylvania, and one of James's students, A. E. Singer Jr., was a famous professor in that Department for many years. Although Singer had already retired when I entered the university, he was still living in Philadelphia, and some senior members of the Department visited him regularly. One of those members, C. West Churchman, wrote the following four principles, which he attributed to Singer, on the blackboard:

- (1) Knowledge of facts presupposes knowledge of theories.
- (2) Knowledge of theories presupposes knowledge of facts.
- (3) Knowledge of facts presupposes knowledge of values.
- (4) Knowledge of values presupposes knowledge of facts.

and I am sure that Singer's teacher, William James, would have agreed!

- (1) is no longer controversial, although it was very much so in James's day (and even some decades after his death, when the idea of "protocol sentences", reports of direct experience uncontaminated by theory, was defended by some members of the Vienna Circle). But (3) is as controversial today as it was then, so I should like to lay out some reasons for accepting it.

One desideratum accepted by both Pragmatists and Neopositivists is *coherence*.[26] But what is a "coherent" body of belief? Mere deductive consistency is hardly enough; although why Positivists require even *that* is not wholly clear. (If the fundamental aim of science is *prediction*, might that aim not be more efficiently reached if we allowed a plurality of theories, each consistent and successful in its own domain, even if their conjunction were not consistent? We could simply disallow the conjunction of statements from different bodies of theory, barring special licence – indeed, this has even been defended by the Princeton philosopher Bas van Fraassen.) The fact is that ¡coherence makes sense as a desideratum precisely because we view our system of knowledge as *more* than just a prediction machine; we aim at a *Weltanschauung*. As James remarks, "An *outrée* explanation, violating all our preconceptions, would never pass for a true account . . . We should scratch around industriously until we found something less eccentric."[27] value something that wont freak us out.

But what is explanatory and what is "outrée" is itself frequently a matter of controversy, even in the hardest science. The present form of quantum mechanics was the product of two conferences at Solveg in the 1930s – and those conferences discussed philosophical issues at least as much as physical ones! Moreover, the quantum mechanical *Weltanschauung* that emerged from the 2nd Solveg Conference – the "Copenhagen Interpretation" – remains controversial even today. A substantial minority of cosmologists have deserted it for the so-called "Many Worlds Interpretation" – an interpretation which implies, among other things, that there are "parallel worlds", including, very probably, ones in which America is still a British Colony, ones in which the Revolution never took place, etc.! To me the Many Worlds Interpretation *is* simply too "outrée", I must admit. But both sides admit that what is at issue is not *prediction*. What is at issue is precisely what is explanatory and what is not, what is coherent and what is not. And when such disputes break out at a fundamental level they always cross boundaries; philosophical issues are mixed with "scientific" ones, and cultural and even metaphysical preconceptions play a role. James describes this situation accurately when he writes:

New truth is always a go-between, a smoother-over of transitions. It marries old opinion to new fact so as to show a minimum of jolt, a maximum of continuity. We hold a theory true just in proportion to its success at solving this problem of "maxima and minima". But success in solving this problem is eminently a problem of approximation. [Compare Quine's "trade-offs".] We say this theory solves it on the whole more satisfactorily than that theory; but that means more satisfactorily to ourselves, and individuals will emphasize their points of satisfaction differently. To a certain degree, therefore, everything here is plastic.[28]

＊ Please note that I am not claiming that the fundamental methodological and philosophical issues that are debated when we make deep changes in our very paradigms of scientific explanation are *ethical* issues, but I am claiming that *value* issues are involved, for the decision as to what *counts* as "coherent" and what counts as "outrée" is in every sense a value judgment.

In physics, at least, empiricist philosophers of science like to claim that we can treat the "observation vocabulary" as fixed, for any physical phenomenon, however *recherché*, must, if demonstrated, make a difference to the motions of some middle-sized objects, such as our familiar dials and photographic plates. (Although historians of science and philosophers of science have reminded us that the description of the motions of those middle-sized objects is invariably theory loaded.) But when we come to the study of human beings, even this much cannot be assumed. We classify people as cruel or compassionate, socially skilled or inept, connoisseurs or tyros, and sometimes with a high degree of intersubjective agreement; yet there is no reason at all to think that these classifications could be reduced to some fixed physicalistic vocabulary.[29] Moreover, some of these classifications are classifications of phenomena whose very existence is partly brought about and sustained *by* the classifications. Daniel Bell has sometimes termed this order of phenomena "the constructed order". For example (this is Bell's example), sex is a biological phenomenon, but gender is a "constructed" phenomenon; whether people are classified as male or female is a matter of biology, but whether they are classified as "maidenly" or "chivalrous" is a matter of culture, and, as we know, behaviors which are aptly classified as "maidenly" or "chivalrous" are unlikely to persist unless the classifications themselves do. Whether they do is hardly independent of the acceptance or rejection of the evaluations that those classifications presuppose. Similarly, it is probable that "feeling sorry" for someone else under some circumstances is a biologically innate capacity, but "being a compassionate individual" is not a possibility in the absence of a culture which classifies human behaviors under such rubrics, and which shares the evaluations implied by such rubrics. There is no "totality of observational facts" fixed in advance to be described; what is there, even at the level of observational fact, will depend partly on what cultures we create, and that means what languages we create. As James put it:

> • I, for my part, cannot escape the consideration, forced upon me at every turn, that the knower is not simply a mirror floating with no foothold anywhere, and passively reflecting an order that he comes upon and finds simply existing. The knower is an actor, and coefficient of the truth on one side, while on the other he registers the truth which he helps to create.[30]

I have argued that James was right (and Singer was right) to think that decisions about "facts" and "value judgments" depend on and condition one another. And if James said that the true may be "expedient in almost any fashion", it was, I suggest, precisely because one cannot foresee in advance *what* considerations may prove relevant to a given question in the long run. As Vivian Walsh has put it, modifying a metaphor of Quine's, "To borrow and adapt Quine's vivid image, if a theory may be black with fact and white with convention, it might well . . . be red with values."[31]

To the four principles James's student Singer enunciated back in the 1940s, he could have added two more, viz.:

wholism →

- (5) Knowledge of facts presupposes knowledge of interpretations.
- (6) Knowledge of interpretations presupposes knowledge of facts.

For talk of testing the system of scientific theory by "testing predictions" makes sense only when a common world and a common language are already in place. To know that you have tested the same prediction that I have tested I must understand what you say; and that means that issues of interpretation and questions of fact also presuppose and condition one another.

Daniel Dennett has recently argued,[32] that an interpretative stance is correct just to the degree that it is optimal for *prediction* – predicting what the interpretee will say and do; but I do not find this view at all plausible. I have, for example, convictions on what Aristotle meant by certain arguments; but I do not claim to be able to predict Aristotle's "dispositions" any better than anyone else. (It is no use saying, "Well, you must be predicting that *if Aristotle spoke present-day English, had read the current philos-*

ophical literature, etc., he would say your interpretation of his argument in present-day language is the correct one," because the hypothetical situation is just too far-fetched for me to believe that the counterfactual makes sense. I don't think Aristotle *had* dispositions to say things in present-day English! And even in the case of contemporaries too, there is a difference between interpreting someone's speech or writing and predicting what their reaction to the interpretation might be. Hostile interpretations, for example – interpretations whose point is to show that the discourse in question is empty, or pompous, or silly, or hypocritical, etc. – are virtually never accepted by the interpretee when they are *correct*. The fact is that while interpretation and prediction depend on one another, interpretation cannot be reduced simply to prediction.[33])

If James's views evoked hostility, both in his lifetime and after, they have always attracted adherents as well. And if I may hazard a guess, the very feature of James's world view I have been pointing to – the vision of fact, theory, value, and interpretation as all interdependent – is one of the sources of that attraction. To some of us, to those of us of what James would call the Pragmatist "temperament", that vision seems simply more *realistic* than the vision of those who try to convince us that the familiar dualisms *must* be correct.

Realism

Earlier in this talk, I mentioned that, in addition to this attack on the dualisms, James's philosophy contains a strong strain of "direct" realism, that is of the doctrine that perception is of objects and events "out there", and not of private "sense data". And I said that Ruth Anna Putnam and I believe that, far from being inconsistent, each of these aspects of James's philosophy presupposes the other, and each is necessary for the proper interpretation of the other. The *Essays on Radical Empiricism*, in which James spells out his theory of perception, constitute the most technical part of James's philosophy (and, not coincidentally, the part that Russell admired so much). Partly because of this technicality, and partly because I do not wish to keep you here all night, I shall not even attempt to spell out the details. (Those of you who are interested can look at the two essays[34] on James in the third part of *Realism with a Human Face*.) But I do want to say a word about the relation between these two elements in James's thought.

Some of you no doubt recall that the attack on *dualités* is today a feature of the thought of Jacques Derrida, but in Derrida's hands (or perhaps I should say "in Derrida's pen", given Derrida's relentless emphasis on *writing*) it turns into a sense of loss of the world, a loss of the "hors texte". To Derrida, any idea that we have access to a common external world is a return to what he calls "a metaphysics of presence", to discredited ideas of incorrigibility and a preconceptual given. It is precisely the fact that James's emphasis on what he calls the "plasticity" of truth, on our role as "coefficients of the truth on the one side", is balanced by the insistence that we share and perceive a common world, by the insistence that "we register the truth which we help to create", which distances him from all forms of scepticism. Indeed, from the earliest of Peirce's Pragmatist writings, Pragmatism has been characterized by *antiscepticism*: Pragmatists hold that *doubt* requires justification just as much as belief (Peirce drew a famous distinction between "real" and "philosophical" doubt); and by *fallibilism*: Pragmatists hold that there are no metaphysical guarantees to be had that even our most firmly-held beliefs will never need revision. That one can be both fallibilistic *and* antisceptical is perhaps *the* basic insight of American Pragmatism.

Now this will seem a delicate (some will say an impossible) balancing act, but it represents the situation in which we live. It may remove some of the air of impossibility if we realize – as Peirce, James, and Dewey all tried to help us realize – that access to a common reality does not require incorrigibility. Just as fallibilism does not require us to doubt *everything*, it only requires us to be prepared to doubt *anything* – if good reason to do so arises! The fact that perception is *sometimes* erroneous does not show that even *non*-erroneous perception is really perception of "appearances". And it may also help if we realize that access to a common reality does not require access to something *preconceptual*. It requires, rather, that we be able to form *shared* concepts.

Some of you may also be reminded of the controversy that swirls around the interpretation of the philosophy of the later Wittgenstein. Just as James tries to "humanize" the notion of truth, to view it (as he views all notions) as a human instrument, and not as an idea that dropped from the sky, Wittgenstein insists that all our notions depend on our "form of life". And there is also a realist element in Wittgenstein's philosophy. I recall once saying (mistakenly) that Wittgenstein would never use a phrase like "correspond to reality" and being brought up short by Cora Diamond, who pointed out that in a lecture on the philosophy of mathematics,[35] Wittgenstein remarks that he *would* say that "This chair is blue" *corresponds to a reality* – although he can only say what reality by using that very sentence. And he reminds us that "the thises and thats we can point to" are our paradigms of reality. And there are those who find this realist strain (if they recognize its presence at all) an inconsistency in Wittgenstein's thought. It may seem strange to compare James to the later Wittgenstein, given Wittgenstein's hostility to metaphysics and James's undeniable metaphysical bent, but it is not entirely unwarranted: indeed, in "The Moral Philosopher and the Moral Life",[36] we find James offering what is clearly an anticipation of Wittgenstein's celebrated Private Language Argument, and defending the proposition that "truth presupposes a standard external to the thinker."

These are immensely hard issues, and I do not wish to give the impression that one can find the "answers" in the work of James or the work of Wittgenstein, or that there are final "answers" at all. But they are worth thinking about, and I find James's way of thinking about them (and, in a different way, Wittgenstein's way of thinking about them) inspiring.

Philosophy and Life

In conclusion, let me say that in the process of defending James from the charge of being an inconsistent thinker, I hope I have not stressed the complexity and depth of his argument to such an extent as to obscure the fact that for James, as for Socrates, the central philosophical question is *how to live*. But for James, as for Socrates and his successors, the opposition between philosophy which is concerned with how to live and philosophy which is concerned with hard technical questions is a false opposition. We want ideals and we want a world view, and we want our ideals and our world view to support one another. Philosophy which is all argument feeds no real hunger; while philosophy which is all vision feeds a real hunger, but it feeds it Pablum. If there is one overriding reason for being concerned with James's thought, it is that he was a genius who was concerned with real hungers, and whose thought, whatever its shortcomings, provides substantial food for thought – and not just for thought, but for life.

Notes

This lecture is a reworked version of a talk I delivered to the American Academy of Arts and Sciences in February 1992.

1. *The Analysis of Mind* (London: George Allen and Unwin, 1921), p. 22.
2. *The WHYS of a Philosophical Scrivener* (New York: William Morrow and Co., 1983).
3. *Ibid.*, p. 45.
4. *A Stroll with William James* (New York: Harper & Row, 1983), p. 5.
5. On the interpenetration of fact and value, see, for example, "The Place of Affectional Facts in a World of Pure Experience" in *Essays in Radical Empiricism* (Cambridge, Mass.: Harvard University Press, 1976), which also attacks the dualism of "inner" and "outer" events. I discuss the interpenetration of fact and theory in the third lecture of the present series; the claim that our conception of any fact involves a conception of lawlike consequences (how the things in question may be expected to behave) was at the heart of Peirce's "pragmatic maxim" cited by James in *Pragmatism*. James also attacks the idea of incorrigible introspective knowledge: "If to *have* feelings or thoughts in their immediacy were enough, babies in the cradle would

be psychologists, and infallible ones. But the psychologist must not only *have* his mental states in their absolute veritableness, but he must report them and write about them, classify and compare them and trace their relations to other things . . . And in the naming, classing, and knowing of things in general we are notoriously fallible, why not also here?" *Principle of Psychology* I (New York: Dover, 1950), pp. 189–190.

6 In a letter to William James, Strong reports that F. C. S. Schiller "wasn't able to understand" James's "A World More About Truth" (reprinted in *The Meaning of Truth*).

7 Some critics even read James – against repeated statements to the contrary, explicit and implicit, in his writing – as holding that if the consequences of believing that *p* are good for *you*, then *p* is "true for you". Let me say once and for all that James never used the notion of "true for me" or "true for you". Truth, he insists, is a notion which presupposes a community, and, like Peirce, he held that the widest possible community, the community of all persons (and possibly even all sentient beings) in the long run, is the relevant one. Note that even Russell, in caricaturing James's position on truth, does not make *this* mistake.

8 Bertrand Russell, *A History of Western Philosophy* (New York: Simon & Schuster, 1945), p. 817.

9 *Pragmatism* and *The Meaning of Truth* (one-volume edition) (Cambridge, Mass.: Harvard University Press, 1978), p. 106. Emphasis in the original.

10 *Philosophical Investigations* §43.

11 Another famous thematic statement is "The true is the name of whatever proves itself to be good in the way of belief, and good, too, for definite assignable reasons" (*Pragmatism*, p. 43). Note that James does not say, "for *any* reasons whatsoever" – he is going to go on and say what those "definite assignable reasons" are – yet he is often read as if he had written "for any reasons whatsoever"!

12 *The Meaning of Truth* – p. 272 in the Harvard one-volume edition cited in n. 9 (106 in the separate volume, also published by Harvard).

13 "Extraordinary fertility in consequences verifiable by sense," *Pragmatism*, p. 91.

14 "We keep unaltered as much of our old knowledge, as many of our old prejudices and beliefs, as we can," *ibid.*, p. 83.

15 "A new belief counts as 'true' just in proportion as it gratifies the individual's desire to assimilate the novel in his experience to his beliefs in stock", *ibid.*, p. 36.

16 *Ibid.*, p. 44.

17 Cf. "Two Dogmas of Empiricism" in Quine's *From A Logical Point of View* (Cambridge, Mass.: Harvard University Press, 1953).

18 In addition, James insists that subjective "satisfaction" is irrelevant unless "reality also be incidentally led to", *The Meaning of Truth*, edition cited, p. 272 [106]. This is, of course, connected with James's realism, discussed below.

19 Cf. Chapter 4 of my *Representation and Reality* for a critical discussion of the claimed philosophical significance of Tarski's work.

20 James is aware of this charge, and he replies to it, *ibid.*, p. 274 [108].

21 Cf. "Spencer's Definition of Mind as Correspondence," in James's *Essays in Philosophy* (Cambridge, Mass.: Harvard University Press, 1978), p. 21. I should add that in this essay (from 1878), James makes it clear that what is "fated" to be thought is not strictly predetermined; the Jamesian doctrine that we help to determine what shall become "coercive over thought" is clearly present in the essay. In *Pragmatism*, truth, in this sense, becomes a "regulative notion" rather than something we are sure of attaining.

22 These were published as an issue of the *Journal of Philosophy* in September 1994. See especially the third lecture, "The Face of Cognition".

23 This is the beginning of James's reponse to the sixth of

seven "misunderstandings of Pragmatism": "*Sixth misunderstanding: Pragmatism explains not what truth is, but only how it is arrived at.*" Cf. *The Meaning of Truth*, edition cited, pp. 274–275 [108–109].

24 This is Chapter VIII of *The Meaning of Truth*.

25 *Ibid.*, p. 266 [100].

26 Note, however, that James's notion of coherence ("what fits every part of life best and combines with the collectivity of experience's demands, nothing being omitted") involves the "fit" of beliefs with the demands of experience and with life, not only with other beliefs.

27 *Pragmatism*, p. 35.

28 On the page cited in the previous note.

29 Cf. my *Reason, Truth and History* (Cambridge: Cambridge University Press, 1983) and John McDowell's "Are Moral Requirements Hypothetical Imperatives," *Proceedings of the Aristotelian Society*, suppl. volume 52 (1978) and "Virtue and Reason," *Monist* 62 (1979).

30 In "Spencer's Definition of Mind as Correspondence," p. 21.

31 Vivian Walsh, "Philosophy and Economics," in *The New Palgrave; a Dictionary of Economics*, vol. 3, ed. J. Eatwell, M. Milgate, and P. Newman (London: Macmillan Press, and New York: Stockton Press), 1987.

32 "Real Patterns," *Journal of Philosophy* 88, no. 1 (1991), pp. 27–51.

33 This is a theme that has been stressed by Jürgen Habermas throughout his philosophical career.

34 "James's Theory of Perception" and (with Ruth Anna Putnam) "William James's Ideas," both reprinted in *Realism with a Human Face*.

35 Lecture XXV in *Wittgenstein's Lectures on the Foundations of Mathematics*, ed. Cora Diamond (Chicago: University of Chicago Press, 1989).

36 In *The Will to Believe and Other Essays* (Cambridge, Mass.: Harvard University Press, 1978).

2

Was Wittgenstein a Pragmatist?

Although my subject today is the pragmatist strain in the philosophy of the later Wittgenstein, my title is, in a way, misleading, for I will be talking as much or more about the relation of Wittgenstein's philosophy to Kant's as about its relation to, say, William James's. Thus this lecture might also have been titled "Was Wittgenstein a Neo-Kantian?"

By means of this double comparison, I hope to combat the prevalent idea that Wittgenstein is simply an "end of philosophy" philosopher, i.e. the idea that the whole "message" of the later philosophy of Wittgenstein is that philosophy is analogous to a neurosis, and that the purpose of Wittgenstein's work is simply to enable us to "stop doing philosophy".

One difficulty in talking about the later philosophy is that Wittgenstein very deliberately refuses to state philosophical theses. His purpose, as he explains, is to change our point of view,[1] not to utter theses. If there were theses in philosophy, he tells us, everyone would recognize them as trivial. Thus, while I can explain something that I think is fundamentally right in the philosophy of, for example,

Rudolf Carnap, by saying that there is something right in Carnap's distinction between framework questions and internal questions, even if Carnap stated that distinction in a way which depends on what Quine called the "two dogmas of empiricism" – and while I can explain some things that I think are lastingly right in the philosophy of Hans Reichenbach by saying that Reichenbach was right in his criticism of Kant's *synthetic a priori*,[2] and that Reichenbach's idea of equivalent descriptions is of lasting value – I cannot simply state a *thesis* of Wittgenstein's which is lastingly right. Nevertheless, I think that seeing how, in a way, Wittgenstein's reflections flow from and continue some of Kant's reflections, and how they parallel a certain strain in pragmatism, may enable us to see better in just what *way* Wittgenstein wishes us to change our point of view, to change the way we see things, and also to see why it is so hard to express that change in the form of a "thesis".

Kant

Let me begin, then, with Kant. If I had to say what was lastingly right in Kant's first Critique – and I myself think there is something lastingly right in every one of Kant's books – I would say that, whatever Kant's mistakes (the synthetic apriori, for example), Kant was the first really to see that describing the world is not simply copying it. Kant saw that whenever human beings describe anything in the world, our description is shaped by our own conceptual choices.[*] By saying that our descriptions of the world are shaped by our own conceptual choices I do not mean merely that they exhibit trivial semantic conventionality, as illustrated by the fact we can describe something by saying that it is one meter long or, alternatively, by saying that it is thirty-nine point so and so many inches long. Kant appreciated that we describe the world for different purposes, for example, for scientific purposes and also for moral purposes, and that neither of these descriptions is reducible to or intertranslatable with the other, although he believed, and I think he was right, that our moral images and our scientific images can both be right.

However, Kant was himself subject to a confusion. The confusion was to suppose that a description which is shaped by our conceptual choices is somehow, for that very reason, not a description of its object "as it really is". As soon as we make *that* mistake, we open the door to the question, "Well, if our descriptions are only *our* descriptions, descriptions shaped by our interests and nature, then what is the description of the things as they are *in themselves?*" But this "in themselves" is quite empty – to ask how things are "in themselves" is, in effect, to ask how the world is to be described in the world's own language, and there is no such thing as the world's own language, there are only the languages that we language users invent for our various purposes. (Indeed, I believe that in the first Critique Kant himself repeatedly comes to the very point of seeing that the notion of a "thing in itself" is empty, and always backs away from his own recognition of that fact; but still, there *is* some recognition of that fact, I would claim, even at moments in the first Critique.) But even though Kant's recognition that our description of the world is shaped by our own conceptual choices, which are in turn shaped by our nature and interests, is marred and flawed – marred, on the one hand, by the notion of the *Ding an sich*, and, on the other, by the notion that our conceptual choices are fixed once and for all by some kind of thick transcendent structure of reason – it does seem to me that Kant made a decisive advance over all previous philosophers in giving up the idea that any description of the world can be simply a copy of the world. •

We know, moreover, that the idea of taking this point from Kant, while scrapping the idea of a transcendent structure of reason which gives rise to a set of apriori categories and synthetic apriori truths, etc., was ubiquitous in German philosophy before Wittgenstein. For example, there was Schopenhauer's replacement of Reason by Will in his own eccentric version of Kantianism, and we know that the young Wittgenstein was deeply influenced by Schopenhauer.

Another fascinating aspect of Kant's thought is what I would call its *incipient* pluralism. I have already alluded to that by referring to the fact that in Kant there is not just one image of the world but two images of the world, a scientific image of the world and a moral image of the world. This might, of course, be termed a dualism rather than a pluralism; but I think we see, especially in the third Critique and in Kant's postcritical writings, a *tendency* towards genuine pluralism, which Kant perhaps resisted, but which nevertheless surfaces in his work. Specifically, instead of seeing the simple dualism of a scientific image of the world and a moral image of the world, we see various interactions between these two and various spin-offs – spinoffs that come from the interdependence of the moral image of the world and the scientific image of the world, which I will speak about in a few minutes; spinoffs that come from the interaction of pure practical reason with sensibility and inclination, and so on. In effect, Kant begins to speak not only of a moral image of the world and a scientific image of the world, but also (in *Religion Within the Bounds of Reason Alone*) of a religious image of the world, one which is subservient to the moral image of the world, but beginning to develop some autonomy of its own; and he also begins to speak (in *The Critique of Judgement*) of what one might call aesthetic images of the world, and also of legal images of the world, and so on. To be sure, Kant, like Quine in our day, continued to insist that only the scientific image of the world contains what can properly be called "knowledge". But this feature of Kant's thought was to be called into question by William James, as well as by the later philosophy of Wittgenstein.

In a sense, then, I can already state one "thesis" of my lecture (you see, I have "theses", even if Wittgenstein doesn't), which is that Wittgenstein's *practice* cannot be understood as a simple *repudiation* of something called "traditional philosophy"; Wittgenstein is as much continuing a tradition of philosophical reflection as he is repudiating certain kinds of philosophical reflection.

To be sure, the moment of repudiation is there in Wittgenstein, it is stark, and it is in a way shocking. Wittgenstein, I would say, tells us that the traditional enterprises of metaphysics and epistemology have failed; and not just that they have failed at the end of the day, but that they failed, so to speak, at the beginning of the day, that they were stillborn, that the questions which are supposed to generate metaphysics and epistemology are, as they are traditionally formulated, nonsensical.[3] Epistemology, for example, is often thought to be generated by the question "What is the nature of knowledge?"; but Wittgenstein, as I read him, wants to tell us that the very assumption that knowledge has a "nature" is one that we have not succeeded in giving a sense. And it will not help to restate it in the formal mode of speech, as, say, "What is the analysis of the concept of knowledge?", or "What is the meaning of the word 'know'?"; because Wittgenstein wants to tell us that the idea (which, today, is still common to both "causal theories of knowledge" and "justified true belief" theories) that the word "know" has a meaning that surrounds it, like an "aura" that accompanies it in all its contexts of use, determining how we use it in those contexts, is an illusion. The word "know" is a word we use to do many different jobs. You can, to be sure, describe various of the jobs that the word "know" performs, but you won't be doing traditional epistemology, or even modern, non-traditional epistemology in the style of Rudolf Carnap. You won't, for example, tell us, nor could you possibly tell us, what the criteria are by which we are to know which uses of "know" in the future will be legitimate or rational, and which uses of "know" in the future will be illegitimate or irrational; for that is not something that anyone can tell us once and for all. Human beings are self-surprising creatures; we have always created new language games, and we shall continue to create new language games; we have always extended and modified the use of the word "know" and we shall continue to extend and modify the use of the word "know".

Rorty and Wittgenstein

Now, what I just said may sound very much like Richard Rorty, and in *Contingency, Irony, Solidarity* Rorty, in fact, presents his views as an extension of those of the later Wittgenstein. As Rorty interprets the ideas that I have just been describing, their upshot is this: we have a variety of language games; what is true and false in a language game is determined by a set of criteria; one can ask what the correct way to use the word "know" is *in a particular language game*, and one can investigate that question using ethnography, or using history of ideas, or using Wittgensteinian language analysis, but all that will give one will be a description of the use of the word in one particular language game. In addition, according to Rorty, there is no such thing as one language game being *better* than another except in the sense of "better relative to certain interests". Of course, Rorty would agree that we will always go on producing new language games, or at least Rorty hopes that that is the case.

This Rortian interpretation of the later philosophy of Wittgenstein, while undeniably influential today, seems to me as much a falsification of Wittgenstein as a clarification of his meaning, although it is close to interpretations that were given some thirty years ago by epigones of Wittgenstein like Norman Malcom; indeed, when I first started doing philosophy, a great deal of my activity was devoted to refuting Malcolm's version of Wittgensteinianism, and my colleague Stanley Cavell spent a great deal of his time trying to show that that point of view, while it may be Malcolm's, was not Wittgenstein's at all. The heart of Rorty's reading is his comparison of criteria with "programs". Ever since he published *Philosophy and the Mirror of Nature*, Rorty has seen what he called "normal" discourse in that book, and what he calls by the Wittgensteinian term "language games" in *Contingency, Irony, Solidarity*, as governed by what he calls "algorithms" or "programs".[4] When we are within "normal discourse", when we are "playing the same language game", we follow programs in our brains and we all agree. That is Rorty's picture.

This picture of language speakers as automata is deeply un-Wittgensteinian, I want to say. I think it is because Rorty sees language games as virtually automatic performances that he regards any normative notion of reason as just metaphysical gobbledygook. If *I* say, for example, that there are better and worse language games, and that human reason is not just one capacity but a large number of capacities which enable us, among other things, to tell which language games are better and worse, then Rorty's reaction is to say that "Putnam has become a metaphysical realist at the end of the day."[5] And indeed, if reason, in the sense in which I have just used the term, were not needed at all to speak within one language game; if reason were something that we needed to invoke only when we philosophers are trying to explain why we sometimes give up a language game and adopt a new one, then it would be a suspect notion. Thus Rorty's picture of "normal discourse" deeply affects his picture of non-normal, or "hermeneutic", discourse.

But this picture of normal discourse, I want to say, is a caricature of our lives with our language. For one thing, people speaking what is in every sense *one* language, not adopting a "new vocabulary" or anything like that, very, very often are unable to come into agreement using the "criteria" they know. For example, Rorty and I both believe, and we think that all reasonable people who read good newspapers closely believe, that there are almost certainly no American prisoners of war still alive in Vietnam. Some people in our country (including, understandably, some relatives of soldiers who were listed as Missing in Action during the Vietnam war) believe that there are American prisoners of war still in Vietnam. Is Rorty going to say that the notion of "objectivity" doesn't apply in such a case? Is he going to say that the two sides

are "playing different language games" and that there is
no objective fact as to whether there are American prisoners of war still in Vietnam? Is he going to say that the
sentence "There are no American prisoners of war still in
Vietnam" is "true in the language game Rorty and I play"
and false in the language game certain others play, and
that is all there is to it? A view which takes seriously the
notion of *programs and algorithms in the brain,* but does not
take seriously the notion that *either there are or aren't
American prisoners of war still in Vietnam* is certainly not to
be equated with anything Wittgenstein ever believed.

Wittgenstein himself is quite clear in pointing out that
language is *not* simply a matter of following rules (like
calculating rules); and not just because rules are not the
"foundation" of language (that is because rules themselves, according to Wittgenstein, rest on what he calls
our "natural reactions"). The points in the text of the
Investigations I want to recall here are the following: on the
one hand, there are, to be sure, parts of language where
we do all normally agree. Normally we do all call very
much the same things red, for example. And we certainly
do not come into disagreement on which *color* red is.
(Sceptical doubt as to whether the color we all *call* "red"
really *is* red is incoherent.) Similarly, we do not come into
disagreement on which operation is adding one to a
number (here I am thinking of numbers that people
actually do write down and add, not numbers six light
years long, or numbers in logically possible worlds, or
what not). In cases that actually arise in our real everyday
lives, we do not disagree about what it is to add one to a
number, or to add two to a number. (And a sceptical
doubt about whether the operation we all *call* "adding
two" really *is* adding two would be dotty.) Wittgenstein
is concerned to make these points – which are not "theses"

but, as he himself says are quite obvious – in order to combat a certain kind of mentalistic mystification about what it is to understand, say, the rule "add two". Although Wittgenstein stresses these cases early on in the *Investigations*, he does not by any means think that all of language is governed by rules like calculating rules: To suppose otherwise is to read carelessly.

Let me quote a passage in which Wittgenstein makes it quite clear that language is not all like that. The context is one in which he imagines that people are having a disagreement about whether someone is pretending to have a feeling that he doesn't have (*Philosophical Investigations*, IIxi, p. 227; I have rectified the translation):

"You don't understand a thing" – so one says when someone doubts what we recognize as clearly genuine, – but we can't prove anything.

"Is there such a thing as 'expert judgment' about the genuiness of expressions of feeling? – Even here there are those whose judgment is 'better' and those whose judgment is 'worse'.

Correcter prognoses will generally issue from the judgments of those who understand people better (*des besseren Menschenkenners*).

Can one learn this knowledge? Yes; some can. Not, however, by taking a course in it, but through 'experience'. – Can another be one's teacher in this? Certainly. From time to time he gives him the right *tip*. This is what 'learning' and 'teaching' are like here. – What one acquires is not a technique; one learns correct judgments. There are also rules, but they do not form a system, and only experienced people can apply them right. Unlike calculating rules."

Here also we see Wittgenstein recognizing quite explicitly that even within one language game there may be truths which not every one can see, because not everyone can develop the skill of recognizing the "imponderable evidence" (*unwägbare Evidenz*, p. 228) involved.[6] Some people are just better at telling what is going on. Nothing could be farther from the picture of a language game as an automatic performance, like the execution of an algorithm. (I neglect here the question of whether *everything* we do, including general intelligence, is "in the last analysis" a matter of executing algorithms, perhaps not at the level of our so-called "performance description" but at the level of our so-called "competence description", because I think that these questions are not relevant to what Rorty is doing. Rorty's notion of a "program" is one which leads to *identical* behavior in all the members of the speech community, whereas general intelligence does not always lead to agreement among all the members of a speech community; and, in any case, I dealt with the whole issue of Functionalism in *Representation and Reality*.)

Not only are there better and worse performances within a language game, but it is quite clear that Wittgenstein thinks that there are better and worse language games. For example, he regards the language games played by philosophers as constraining: philosophers are "in the grip of a picture"; they are talking nonsense. At the same time he is much more generous to other kinds of non-philosophical language and to other kinds of non-scientific language games, especially the language games of "primitive" people. (But, although he by no means shares the usual Western progressivist view that pre-literate people are simply in the stage of pre-science or pseudo-science or superstition, he does indicate that there are some primitive language games that he would "combat" and some primitive language games that he finds "absurd".[7] He mentions, for example, ordeal by fire.)

To pull this together, then, Rorty's reading of Wittgenstein is one from which very radical theses follow, for example, that there is no such thing as one language game being better than another, there is only being better *relative to this, that, or the other interest*, and that we cannot say (according to Rorty) that Newton's physics is superior to Aristotle's physics, or that there are things that Aristotle's physics got wrong and that Newton's physics got right.[8] None of these theses should be read into Wittgenstein. Nevertheless, I do want to say that although Rorty's reading is not right, it does catch a real feature of Wittgenstein's view. Wittgenstein inherits and extends what I above called Kant's pluralism; that is the idea that no one language game deserves the *exclusive* right to be called "true", or "rational", or "our first-class conceptual system",[9] or the system that "limns the ultimate nature of reality", or anything like that. Wittgenstein, so to speak, splits the difference between Rorty and Quine; that is, he agrees with Rorty, against Quine, that one cannot say that scientific language games are the only language games in which we say or write truths, or in which we describe reality; but, on the other hand, he agrees with Quine as against Rorty that language games can be criticized (or "combatted"); that there are better and worse language games.[10]

More about Wittgenstein and Kant

I want now to return to the question of the relation
between the later philosophy of Wittgenstein and Kant's.
I shall shortly focus on an aspect of that relation that has
not yet been mentioned; but, for the moment let me say
something about the differences between Wittgenstein and
Kant in the areas that we have so far discussed. Some of
them are obvious: Wittgenstein, as I already said, drops
the notion of the thing in itself, drops the synthetic apriori,
drops the table of categories, and so on. One might say
that Wittgenstein "naturalizes" Kantianism (this has also
been said of William James). But what does the "naturalization" here consist in? "Naturalize" is a dangerous word;
especially today, when "naturalism" is often connected
with reductive versions of physicalism; and Wittgenstein
is no reductionist. The "naturalization" is, perhaps, best
described as a *deflation*. It is natural to describe Kant's view
by saying that we can't describe the world as it is in itself;
and, indeed, this is the way Rorty repeatedly states one of
his (as he thinks) points of agreement with Wittgenstein.
But Wittgenstein, true to his strategy of not offering
"theses", tries to convince us that there is no interesting
thesis in this area. For Wittgenstein, the negation of a
pseudo-proposition is a pseudo-proposition; the negation
of nonsense is nonsense. If we are persuaded that it is
unintelligible to say "We sometimes succeed in describing
reality as it is in itself", then we should realize that it is
equally unintelligible to say "We never succeed in describing reality as it is in itself", and even more unintelligible
(more, because it introduces the peculiar philosophical
"can't") to say "We *can't* describe reality as it is in itself".
This great Rortian thesis is the illusion of a truth, the

illusion of a cosmic discovery. In fact, one might say that it is characteristic of Wittgenstein to try to show us that when philosophers say that we *can't* do something, say that something is *impossible*, typically the thing that they tell us it is impossible to do is a nonsense thing, an unintelligible thing; that the philosopher, as it were, seems to be telling us of an Impotence, in the way the physicist tells us of an Impotence when he says "You can't build a perpetual motion machine", or of a barrier we can't cross, but it turns out on examination that the barrier is a mirage, or even less than a mirage – that it is chimerical. We can learn and change and invent languages, and in them we can state truths; that *is* describing reality. If you say, "Yes, but it is not describing reality as it is in itself", you are saying *nothing*. Indeed, Wittgenstein himself may have fallen prey to the temptation to say that we *can't* do something which it makes no sense to do in the famous last line of the *Tractatus*. To say that whereof we cannot speak, thereof we *must* be silent is precisely to say that we mustn't try to express . . . *what?* (James Conant has recently suggested that this is a deliberate contradiction;[11] that the *Tractatus* puts itself into the abyss in this way in order to make exactly the point that I am making now.)

In sum, there is an enormous difference between Kantian *tone*, which Rorty retains by saying that we *can't* describe reality as it is in itself, and the Wittgensteinian tone which is to try to make his reader *not want to say* either "we can describe reality as it is in itself" or "we can't describe reality as it is in itself". Even the profound-sounding remark I made in my own way a little while ago, that there are truths which don't belong to what Quine would call our "first-class conceptual scheme" which are nonetheless fully intelligible and true, is, in a way, deflated for me by reading Wittgenstein; deflated by the fact that he gives very trivial examples. For example, if I give someone the instruction "Stand roughly here", and I later describe what happened by saying "I told him to stand roughly there, and then I took his picture", I certainly "say what is true", and yet "He stood roughly there" is hardly something that belongs to Quine's "first-class conceptual scheme". Again, instead of saying that we have "a moral image of the world and a scientific image of the world", as a neo-Kantian might, Wittgenstein simply says that ethical words are also words which have uses in our language.

This aspect of Wittgenstein's practice, that he wants to make his new philosophical point of view seem *homely* to us; seem not a matter of philosophical theses, but of evident facts that we have known all along, reminds me at times (as it has reminded Stanley Cavell) of one side of American transcendentalism, the side expressed by Thoreau when he says that "there is a solid bottom everywhere"[12] (although, of course, it lies under a fearful amount of mud). Wittgenstein, after all, describes his aim, in a passage worthy of Thoreau, as "to bring our words back to their *home* in the language" (emphasis added).

In spite of these differences – and they are profound – between Wittgenstein and Kant, I want to repeat that, even if you are as critical of the *practice* of philosophers as Wittgenstein is, you can see that a great metaphysician like Kant is not just someone who made some great, if very profound, mistakes; one must also say that there are some genuine insights in Kant, insights which were hard-won, and by which Wittgenstein himself was educated. Wittgenstein could not have seen so far if he had not stood on the shoulders of that giant.

The primacy of practical reason

But there is another side to Kant's thought, a side that connects immediately with pragmatism: the side that we might call *the primacy of practical reason*. It is clear to students of Kant's work that a great deal of that work had a directly political inspiration, as well as a political application. Even the central notion of "self-legislation" that Kant uses in the second Critique and in the *Foundation of the Metaphysics of Morals* was, after all, directly inspired by Rousseau; and in the age of Kant, the idea that a society should be a free union of self-legislating citizens was a revolutionary idea. But I want to mention a different aspect of the primacy of practical reason in Kant, and this is Kant's famous claim (in the Doctrine of Method section of the *Critique of Pure Reason*) that theoretical understanding would not by itself have given us the idea of science as a *unified system of laws* (by which I take it that Kant means we would not even have arrived at Newtonian physics, let alone the regulative ideal of an eventual science that would subsume physics, biology, etc.), that it would not have taken us beyond knowledge of individual inductive generalizations by itself. To get the kind of knowledge represented by Newton's system of the world (or we might say today, by Einstein's system of the world, or by quantum mechanics) one needs what Kant called *the regulative idea of Nature*. That is, you need the vision of nature as governed not just by individual laws, but by a system of laws. That vision, Kant tells us, does not come from theoretical reason, but from *pure practical reason*. Kant was saying that the norms which guide theoretical science in its greatest achievements are norms which derive from a certain notion we have of what the perfection of human inquiry would be, from a certain image of human flourishing in the theoretical realm. (This is something that I myself have argued in *Reason, Truth and History*; that is to say, that our cognitive ideals only make sense considered as part of our idea of human flourishing.)

This idea of the primacy of practical reason, extends, for Kant, to philosophy itself. We cannot, Kant thinks, construct a moral image of the world by seeking to prove apriori that there are true value judgments. The famous Kantian strategy is the other way around (although today philosophers like Bernard Williams often forget this when they are criticizing Kant). The strategy is to say: As a being who makes value judgments every day, I am *of course* committed to the idea that there are true value judgments; *what must be the case if there are to be true value judgments?* In what kind of a world can there be true value judgments?

If you put Kant's strategy that way, you find the same strategy, though not the apriorism, in the writings of John Dewey.[13] I think that this idea of the primacy of practical reason (though not of "pure" practical reason) is a terribly important one *now* for the following reason: At the time of the Vienna Circle, it looked very easy to be an anti-metaphysician. To be an anti-metaphysician all you had to do was confine knowledge to the prediction and control of observables. And everybody knew what an "observable" was. In effect, you were either a 'metaphysician" or you were an "empiricist". The problem with that is that it quickly became obvious, as it did to me, for example, when I first entered the profession, that Mach and his followers in the Vienna Circle had simply exchanged one metaphysics for another. They rightly saw that to argue about whether electrons "really exist" was to argue about a pseudo-question, and then they proceeded to say that to say that electrons exist just *means* that observables behave in such and such a way, without seeing that they, in effect, had simply asserted the pseudo-thesis of phenomenalism in order to defeat the pseudo-thesis of transcendent realism. Saying that when I say that electrons are flowing through a wire I am talking about observables is just as much being a metaphysician (perhaps a Berkeleyan metaphysician) as saying that electrons are things in themselves. This realization, that positivism was itself a metaphysics – and, indeed, an unbelievable one (why should I believe the world consists only of observables, after all?) – has led, however, to a plethora of metaphysical theories, including metaphysical theories in Princeton, New Jersey, according to which other possible worlds are just as real as our actual world. Questions which even the Middle Ages did not take seriously, such as, for example, Do Numbers Really Exist, are the subject of books and papers today. At least two books on these questions by good philosophers of mathematics have come out in the last five years. Yet it is hard to understand in what way this sort of philosophy can be subject to any kind of control at all, or, indeed, what the questions mean. Grown men and women arguing about whether the number three "really exists" is a ludicrous spectacle. It was in a similar context that John Dewey suggested that the primary task of philosophy should not be this kind of metaphysics, that is, the attempt to construct "a theory of everything", but should rather be criticism of culture. Kant's philosophy, in spite of its metaphysical excesses, was intended as a criticism of culture, as a sketch or plan for an enlightened society making progress towards a state in which social justice, as measured by the formula that reward would be proportional to virtue, would reign.[14] Now, it may seem strange to argue that Wittgenstein's philosophy also has a moral purpose, especially since it is often seen as just a kind of disinterested therapy born of a disgust with theoretical philosophy. But I want to close by arguing that Wittgenstein's philosophy too has a moral purpose, and that it exhibits in a different way the same theme, the primacy of practical reason, that Kant's philosophy does, although in a characteristically deflationary fashion.

The ethical aim of Wittgenstein's later philosophy[15]

To explain why I think there is a "primacy of practical reason" hidden in Wittgenstein's later philosophy (and, for that matter, not only in his *later* philosophy[16]), I need to say a few words more about how I interpret that later philosophy. Since I need to be brief, I will proceed by contrasting my own reading with one as different as possible: this is a way of reading Wittgenstein suggested by Michael Williams[17] and by Paul Horwich.[18] Since Horwich's view is developed at greater length, I shall focus on *it*.

On Horwich's view, a language game is to be understood as consisting of sentences for which (if we confine attention to assertoric language) there are "assertability conditions". These conditions specify that under certain observable conditions a sentence counts as true or at least as "confirmed". (Think of these conditions as stipulating that under certain observable conditions we are allowed to utter certain noises, or write certain marks, and also to expect certain observable events or certain reactions from others.) This model is obviously very similar to Carnap's or Reichenbach's models of a speaker-hearer of a natural language.[19] The key idea (as in Positivism) is that if you know under what conditions a statement is confirmed, you understand the statement. "Truth" is to be understood "disquotationally": to say that a statement is true is just to make an equivalent statement. (More precisely, the "Tarski biconditionals" tell us all we need to know about the notion of truth.) Note that this account differs from Rorty's only in that the "criteria" which govern our use of words provide (in some cases) for degrees of assertability less than certainty. Still, speakers who understand their language in the same way and who have the same evidence should all agree on the degree of assertability of their sentences, in this model, just as in Rorty's.

The assumption that underlies this picture is that the use of words can be described in terms of what speakers are allowed to say and do in observable situations. "Use" is a theoretical notion, and there is a standard way of describing the use of expressions in an arbitrary language game. Let me call this *the positivistic interpretation of Wittgenstein.*

A very different interpretation (one suggested, or very nearly suggested,[20] by Peter Winch in *The Idea of a Social Science*) is the following: the use of the words in a language game cannot be described without using concepts which are related to the concepts employed *in* the game. Winch has discussed the case of the language games of "primitive" peoples; but I believe the same point applies to scientific language games. Consider, for example, the language game of a good electrician. He learns to use such sentences as that old positivist favorite, "current is flowing through the wire". On the positivistic interpretation of Wittgenstein, Wittgenstein must hold (with Bridgeman and early Carnap) that the electrician understands this sentence by knowing that, e.g., it is assertable if the voltmeter needle is deflected, and he recognizes that something is a voltmeter by recognizing that it has a certain appearance (and it has VOLTMETER printed on it, perhaps).

We have already seen what is wrong with this picture in our discussion of Rorty. A good electrician relies on "criteria" in this sense, to be sure; but when things go wrong (and anyone who has ever repaired his own appliances or fixed a car knows how much can go wrong when one is dealing with the real world) he also knows to distrust the critera, and the knowledge of when to distrust the criteria is not itself something which is learned by rules. Rather, we can say here what Wittgenstein said in the passage I quoted earlier about learning to tell if another person is feigning a feeling they do not have:

> Can one learn this knowledge? Yes; some can. Not, however, by taking a course in it, but through "*experience*". – Can another be one's teacher in this? Certainly. From time to time he gives him the right *tip*. This is what "learning" and "teaching" are like here. – What one acquires is not a technique; one learns correct judgments. There are also rules, but they do not form a system, and only experienced people can apply them right. Unlike calculating rules.

I want to apply to this case a remark that Habermas makes at a number of points in *The Theory of Communicative Action*:[21] someone who does not see the "point" of the language game, and who cannot imaginatively put himself in the position of an engaged player, cannot judge whether the "criteria" are applied *reasonably* or unreasonably here. Someone who described the game by saying that the players (the electricians) make certain noises in certain observable situations would not be able to make head or tail of what is going on.

On the other hand, consider the following description of the use of "electricity is flowing through the wire": "One uses a voltmeter, etc., to tell if electricity is flowing through the wire. A voltmeter is constructed in such and such a way —— (here, imagine an explanation of how a voltmeter 'works' – *not* in observation language). In using a voltmeter it is important to be sure that no electromagnetic fields be present which might affect the accuracy of its readings . . ."

Knowing the "use" of "current is flowing through the wire" is knowing things like *this*. Of course, much else is presupposed; in fact, acculturation in a technical society, with all that that entails. *Understanding a language game is sharing a form of life.* And forms of life cannot be described in a fixed positivistic meta-language, whether they be scientific, religious, or of a kind that we do not have in Western industrial societies today.

Note that, on this reading of Wittgenstein, the famous remark[22] that, in a large class of cases, we may say that the meaning of a word is its use in the language is not a *theory* of meaning (although it is the expression of a point of view from which one can question whether one knows what it means to ask for a "theory of meaning", in any sense in which a "theory of meaning" might be metaphysically informative).

Two more points, and I am ready to return to "the primacy of practice". (1) To know under what conditions a statement (not a "sentence") is assertable is to know under what conditions it is true or liable to be true. The idea that assertability conditions are conditions for making a *noise* is a total distortion of Wittgenstein's meaning.

"Assertability" and "truth" are internally related notions: one comes to understand both by standing inside a language game, seeing its "point",[23] and *judging* assertability and truth. (2) Michael Williams has tried to deflect the criticism that this sort of "Wittgensteinianism" is naively positivistic by saying that he rejects the fact/value dichotomy (as I do), and that this permits him to add that *assertability conditions can themselves be reformed.* But this addition employs the notion of "reforming" a language game as though that were *one* fixed notion available to the theorist. To know what counts as a reform in the language game of the electrician one must know the point of his game: to figure out how circuits are behaving, and how to repair them when they need repairing, or to install them, or to design them. If you think of the language game as nothing but a game of making noises in certain observable situations in the hope that making those noises will help you get the lights to go on, then the only notion of "reforming" the rules you will be able to give is a narrowly positivistic one: in effect, we will be back to "the aim of science is prediction and control". While that may look plausible in the case of applied electricity, it will give you no understanding at all of most human language. (In general, as I remarked in *Reason, Truth and History*, the purposes of a language game are not statable without using the language of that game or a related game.)

If this is true even of scientific language, where these ideas become especially important in understanding Wittgenstein is when we turn to Wittgenstein's various discussions of forms of language other than scientific; to his discussion of religious language, of "primitive" language games, and of differing "forms of life" in *On Certainty*. In the "Lectures on Religious Belief", Wittgenstein makes it clear that he, standing outside religious language (or affecting to), cannot say that religious language is cognitive or non-cognitive; all he can say is that, from the "outsiders'" perspective, the religious man is "using a picture". But he adds that in saying this he is not saying that the religious man is *only* using a picture, or only "expressing an attitude". I take Wittgenstein to be saying here that (1) the possibilities of "external" understanding of a deeply different form of life are extremely limited; and (2) that religious claims are not simply badly formulated "empirical" claims. Yet they are not rejected by Wittgenstein out of hand, as are metaphysical claims. So what is going on?

It is here that I detect a moral as well as a philosophical purpose in Wittgenstein's writing. Wittgenstein is urging a certain kind of empathetic understanding. (As he explicitly does in his "Remarks on Frazer's *Golden Bough*".)[24] Wittgenstein thinks that secular Europeans see all other forms of life as "pre-scientific" or "unscientific" and that this is a vulgar refusal to appreciate difference. The reason I think that these concerns of Wittgenstein go to the heart of his philosophy is this: To me the remarks near the end of *On Certainty* about our relationship to other forms of life, as well as the Lectures on Religious Belief and the remarks on Frazer's *Golden Bough* just mentioned, are a declaration that the language philosopher cannot *qua* philosopher tell us whether the putative "statements" made in a form of life very different than the scientific *are* statements or not; I can say "I would never talk like that", or, on the contrary, I can make a form of life my own. But this is not something that philosophy can decide for me. (On this interpretation, Wittgenstein's rejection of metaphysics is a *moral* rejection: metaphysical pictures are *bad* for us, in Wittgenstein's view.) The question, the one we are faced with over and over again, is whether a form of life has practical or spiritual value. But the value of a form of life is not, in general, something one can express in the language games of those who are unable to share its evaluative interests.

This sounds like pragmatism. But it is not the mythical pragmatism (which the real pragmatists all scorned) which says "It's true (for you) if it is good for you". It is much closer to the attitude that Dewey expressed when he wrote:

[Philosophy's] primary concern is to clarify, liberate, and extend the goods which inhere in the naturally generated functions of experience. It has no call to create a world of "reality" *de novo*, nor to delve into secrets of Being hidden from common sense and science. It has no stock of information or body of knowledge peculiarly its own; if it does not always become ridiculous when it sets up as a rival of science, it is only because a particular philosopher happens to be also, as a human being, a prophetic man of science. Its business is to accept and to utilize for a purpose the best available knowledge of its own time and place. And this purpose is criticism of beliefs, institutions, customs, policies with respect to their bearing upon good. This does not mean their bearing upon *the* good, as something itself formulated and attained within philosophy. For as philosophy has no private store of knowledge or of methods for attaining truth, so it has no private access to good. As it accepts knowledge of facts and principles from those competent in science and inquiry, it accepts the goods that are diffused in human experience. It has no Mosaic or Pauline authority of revelation entrusted to it. But it has the authority of intelligence, of criticism of these common and natural goods . . .[25]

In the third of these three lectures, I shall say more about Dewey, and about the way in which this conception of philosophy is worked out by him. Today I have tried to show that, even if Wittgenstein was not in the strict sense either a "pragmatist" nor a "neo-Kantian" he shares with pragmatism a certain Kantian heritage (which William James, too, was extremely loathe to acknowledge), and he also shares a central – perhaps *the* central – emphasis with pragmatism: the emphasis on the primacy of practice.

Notes

1 Cf. *Philosophical Investigations* §9.
2 Cf. Reichenbach's *The Theory of Relativity and Apriori Knowledge* (Los Angeles: The University of California Press, 1965) – German original published in 1920.
3 I say that they are nonsensical "as traditionally formulated" because I do not wish to say, and I do not wish to interpret Wittgenstein as saying, that there is no point in reflecting on these questions. On this, see James Conant's Introduction to the collection of my papers that he edited, *Realism with a Human Face*.
4 Thus Rorty writes, "The world does not speak. Only we do. The world can, *once we have programmed ourselves with a language*, cause us to hold beliefs." Cf. his *Contingency, Irony, and Solidarity* (Cambridge: Cambridge University Press, 1989), p. 6. Compare also the reference to the standards of a community (in "normal" discourse) as "algorithms" in his *Philosophy and the Mirror of Nature* (Princeton: Princeton University Press, 1979), p. 342.
5 See his "Solidarity or Objectivity" in C. West and

J. Rajchman (eds.), *Postanalytic Philosophy* (New York: Columbia University Press, 1985).

6 "It is certainly possible to be convinced by evidence that someone is in such-and-such a state of mind, for instance that he is not pretending. But 'evidence' here includes imponderable evidence" (*Philosophical Investigations*, IIxi, p. 228).

7 See §605 in *On Certainty*.

8 Suppose a terrestrial rock were transported to the moon and released. Aristotle's physics clearly implies that it would fall to the earth, while Newton's physics gives the correct prediction (that it would stay on the moon, or fall to the surface of the moon if lifted and released). There is a certain magnificent indifference to *detail* in saying grandly that Aristotle's physics and Newton's are "incommensurable".

9 This is Quine's term for (properly formalized) science.

10 I say this even though, at first blush, support for Rorty's reading might seem to come from the following passages in *On Certainty*.

§608: Is it wrong for me to be guided in my actions by the propositions of physics? Am I to say that I have no good grounds for doing so? Isn't it precisely this that we call a "good ground"?

§609: Suppose that we met people who did not regard this as a good ground, and who did not regard that as a telling reason. Now how do we imagine this? Instead of the physicist, they consult an oracle. And for that we consider them primitive.

Is it wrong for them to consult an oracle and be guided by it? – If we call this "wrong", aren't we using our language game as a base from which to *combat* theirs?

§610: And are we right or wrong to combat it. Of course there are all sorts of slogans which will be used to support our proceeding.

§611: Where two principles really do meet which

cannot be reconciled with one another, each declares the other a fool and a heretic.

§612: I said I would "combat" the other man. But wouldn't I give him reasons? Certainly, but how far do they go? At the end of *reasons* comes *persuasion*. (Think what happens when missionaries convert natives.)

But on closer reading, the Rortian interpretation is not supportable. First of all, notice one small point. If all we had was §609, then one might say that Wittgenstein was distancing himself from those who say that consulting an oracle is "wrong". It is not clear that the "we" in "if we call this wrong aren't we using our language game as a base from which to combat theirs" includes Wittgenstein himself. But this ambiguity is immediately removed in §612, when Wittgenstein says "I said I would 'combat' the other man". So Wittgenstein isn't just an onlooker here. Wittgenstein himself will at least sometimes combat a different language game. Who wouldn't? (What decent person wouldn't combat a language game that involved ordeal by fire, for example?) And we cannot suppose that the things that Wittgenstein would say if he were combatting another language game (e.g., that it is "absurd" to try to reach a verdict on anything by ordeal by fire) are in some sense not believed by Wittgenstein, or that they are given a special metaphysical reinterpretation by Wittgenstein, for the whole burden of *On Certainty* is that we have no other place to stand but within our own language game. If words like "know", for example, cannot bear a metaphysical emphasis, as Wittgenstein suggests in one place, that is all the more reason for using them where they belong and without that metaphysical emphasis. Wittgenstein simply thinks it absurd to settle questions by ordeal by fire.

Well, what about the end of §612, "But wouldn't I give him reasons? Certainly, but how far do they go? At the end of *reasons* comes *persuasion*. (Think what happens when missionaries convert natives.)"? I take Wittgenstein here to be simply telling us what is the case; that when we try to argue with, say, the Azande, there are times when we cannot find reasons that are reasons for them; the world views are so totally different that we sometimes find that in an argument with an intelligent Azande we cannot resort to ordinary argument based on premises that we share with the Azande but have to resort to persuasion.

11 See his "Must we Show What We Cannot Say?" in *The Senses of Stanley Cavell* (Lewisburgh, Pennsylvania: Bucknell University Press, 1989).

12 *Walden*, Chapter xviii, par. 14. But Thoreau also writes, in the same paragraph, "We read that the traveler asked the boy if the swamp before him had a hard bottom. The boy replied that it had. But presently the traveler's horse sunk in up to the girths, and he observed to the boy, 'I thought you said the swamp had a hard bottom.' 'So it is', said the boy, 'but you have not got half way to it yet.' So it is with the bags and quicksands of society; but he is an old boy that knows it." For Cavell's discussion see Chapter 3 ("Portions") of his *The Senses of Walden* (Viking Press, 1972 and North Point Press, expanded edition, 1981).

13 Cf. my "Pragmatism and Moral Objectivity," in Martha Nussbaum and Jonathan Glover (eds.), *Women, Culture and Equality: A Study in Human Capabilities* (Oxford: Clarendon Press, 1994); collected in my *Words and Life* (Cambridge, Mass.: Harvard University Press, 1994).

14 For a discussion, see Yirmiyahu Yovel, *Kant and the Philosophy of History* (Princeton: Princeton University Press, 1986).

15 In this section I draw on material from "Does the Disquotational Theory of Truth Solve All Philosophical Problems," collected in my *Words and Life*. See also "Sense, Nonsense and the Senses", my Dewey Lectures (published in the *Journal of Philosophy* September 1994), especially lecture 3, "The Face of Cognition."

16 In a letter to a publisher, Ludwig von Ficker, Wittgenstein described the purpose of the *Tractatus* as delimiting "the ethical" *von Innen her*. See von Wright's introduction to the *Prototractatus* (Ithaca: Cornell University Press, 1971), p. 15.

17 I am thinking of Michael Williams's discussion-review of my *Reason, Truth and History* (*Journal of Philosophy* LXXXI, no. 5, May 1984).

18 See Paul Horwich's "Wittgenstein and Kripke on the Nature of Meaning", *Mind and Language*, vol. 5, no. 2 (Summer 1990), and his recent *Truth* (Oxford: Blackwell, 1990).

19 I analyzed those models in "Dreaming and Depth Grammar," reprinted in my *Mind, Language and Reality* (Cambridge University Press, 1975). See pp. 320–324.

20 I say "very nearly suggested" because there is a tendency in Winch – one against which he struggles, to be sure – to regard the language games of primitive peoples as *incommensurable* with ours. This is no part of what Wittgenstein believed. But Winch deserves the credit for having seen much more clearly than almost any other interpreter what Wittgenstein was driving at. In this respect, the essays by Winch collected together as *Ethics and Action* are much superior to *The Idea of a Social Science*.

21 For example, p. 114ff.

22 §43 of the *Investigations*.

23 Cf. §563–4 of *Philosophical Investigations*.

24 L. Wittgenstein, "Remarks on Frazer's *Golden Bough*," in James Klagge and Alfred Nordman (eds.), *Philosophical Occasions: 1912–1951* (Indianapolis: Hackett Publishing Company, 1933), pp. 118–155.

25 John Dewey, *Experience and Nature* (Chicago: Open Court, 1926), pp. 407–408.

3

Pragmatism and the Contemporary Debate

We have seen that the holistic interdependence of fact, value and theory is a central theme in the writing of William James. I have sometimes used the term "interpenetration" in these lectures, to emphasize that the interdependence of which I speak is *not* an interdependence of elements which can always be distinguished, even notionally. To be sure, if I say "beating children is wrong" then, by established usage, if you like, I have made a "value judgment", while if I say "my umbrella is in the closet" I have stated a "fact" – but what if I say "Caligula was a cruel emperor"? Here I have both made a value judgment and stated a historical fact.[1] Or again, if I say "In the 1940s, Walter Gieseking played unaccompanied Bach and Mozart piano music with an amazing sensitivity to all the nuances, and without a trace of inappropriate bravura" I have described Gieseking's playing and, as we say, expressed my appreciation[2] of it.

Philosophers of science have sometimes distinguished between "observations" and "inductive generalizations",[3] while others[4] advocated a three-fold contrast between observations, inductive generalizations, and "abductions", i.e. explanatory theories which go beyond mere inductive generalization. The former dichotomy, between observational data and inductive generalizations, cannot be an absolute one because data statements always presuppose a background of "laws" for their intelligibility. Even phenomenalists pointed this out: I recall C. I. Lewis saying, in his lectures on Theory of Knowledge at Harvard in 1948, that when I say "I see a chair" I am committed to such generalizations as "If I move my eyes right, the visual image will be displaced to the left". And talk of "visual images" aside, I am certainly committed to such "laws" as "If I pick up a chair, other things being equal,[5] it will not be weightless"; "If I sit down on a chair, other things being equal, I will be supported", as well as to a host of assumptions that are so "pivotal" that it would normally be a meaningless speech act to even state them, for example, "It will not turn into a hippopotamus if I smile at it." (As Wittgenstein says in *On Certainty*, such assumptions are like hinges on which a door turns; the rest of the language game would not function without these – unless, of course, we found something to replace these particular "hinges". But then the new "hinge propositions" would play the same role.) Speaking of "interdependence" conveys the fact that the statement "I see a chair" depends for its *justification* on a host of "laws", but it does not point out that the very *content* of the statement is not sharply distinguishable from those laws.[6] That is what I am calling *interpenetration*.

The Peircean contrast, between data and abductive "hypotheses", is not absolute (as Peirce himself well knew) because, in theoretical science, abductive theories can play the role of "hinge propositions".

An amusing but instructive example of the sad consequences of neglecting this interpenetration of fact and theory occurs at the beginning of Ian Hacking's *Representing and Intervening*.[7] Hacking argues that we should be nonrealists with respect to theories (which are just calculating devices, according to him) and realists with respect to what we can "manipulate", either literally or with the aid of instruments. And in a well-known passage, he includes positrons in the class of things we can manipulate. Hacking is describing[8] an experiment in which the charge initially placed on a supercooled niobium ball is gradually changed:

"Now how does one alter the charge on the niobium ball? 'Well, at that stage,' said my friend, 'we spray it with positrons to increase or decrease the charge.' From that day forth I've been a scientific realist. *So far as I am concerned, if you can spray them then they are real*" [emphasis in the original].

Now what does it mean to believe that "they" are "real"? If it means that one believes that there are *distinct things* called "positrons", then we are in trouble – a *lot* of trouble – with the theory. For the theory – quantum field theory – tells us that positrons do not in general have a definite *number*! In the particular experimental setup Hacking is describing, they do have a definite number, perhaps, but it would be quite possible to set up an experiment in which one "sprayed" the niobium ball, not with three positrons, and not with four positrons, but with *a superposition of three and four positrons*. And elementary quantum mechanics already tells us that we cannot think of positrons as having *trajectories* or as being, in general, *reidentifiable*.

If being "a scientific realist" does not mean believing

that positrons exist as distinct *things*, what content is the notion supposed to have? If, on the other hand, it does mean believing that they are things in the sense of having continuous identities, position in space and time, number, etc. – and, as Wittgenstein reminds us,[9] our paradigm of what is "real" is what we can *point to*, and what we can point to certainly has continuous identity, position, can be counted, etc. – then being a "scientific realist" about positrons means believing quantum field theory is actually *false*, and not just interpreting it "nonrealistically" (whatever *that* means). But then, we lose all power to understand just the characteristic quantum phenomena of interference, nonlocality, etc.

I suspect that this is not what Hacking wants, however. I suspect that Hacking wants to say that *here*, in *this* experiment, positrons are "real" *without saying what* that *means*. In Hacking's prose, "real" is just a comforting *noise*, stripped of all its conceptual connections with reidentifiability, countability, locatability, etc. Even Bohr would not deny that a realist *picture* of positrons as separate pellets that one can "spray" is appropriate to *some* experiments (that's what Complementarity is all about); but it is because we have to use different pictures in different experiments that we cannot *just* say "positrons are real" as if that were a self-interpreting statement.

I do not, of course, wish to say that positrons aren't real. But believing that positrons are real has conceptual content only because we have a conceptual scheme – a very strange one, one which we don't fully "understand", but a successful one nonetheless – which enables us to know what to say when about positrons, when we can picture them as objects we can spray and when we can't. Hacking's attempt to draw a sharp line between fact and theory, and to say that one should be a realist about the facts and a nonrealist about the theories, founders on precisely the interpenetration of fact and theory. As James might have put it, the word "positron" isn't a *copy* of a reality, but a "notation", and it is the *theory* that instructs us in the use of the notation. Again the theory and the fact (positrons were sprayed) are not even notionally separable.

When I spoke of "interpretation" in the first lecture, I had in mind the interpretation of linguistic utterances. That "fact" (in the sense of observational data) and "interpretation" (in this sense) are interdependent should be clear, although it has been contested by Quine (of all people!). To know that a prediction has been verified/not verified I must first of all be able to *understand* the prediction, that is, interpret the linguistic expression in question. All talk of "confirmation" in a public activity like science (one, moreover, which is conducted in many different languages and dialects) presupposes interpretation.

Quine[10] rejects this argument on the grounds that observation statements allegedly possess "intersubjective stimulus meaning", and this "stimulus meaning" (which can be determined behavioristically, without any hermeneutical worries, according to Quine) suffices to determine their meaning for scientific purposes. For example, the fact that we can't tell whether the word *gavagai* in a hypothetical "jungle language" means *rabbit* or *undetached rabbit parts* without using "analytic hypotheses" – i.e., an interpretation – is irrelevant, according to Quine, since, as observation reports, these are equivalent.

What is wrong with this claim is that sentences which are "prompted" by the same stimuli need not be alike in truth value. If a tribe says *bosorkanyok* when they see an ugly old woman with a wart on her nose, should we translate this as "ugly old woman with a wart on her nose" or as "witch"?[11] If they expect a "bosorkanyok" and one appears (according to them), did they make a true prediction or a false accusation of witchcraft? The answer requires interpretation of the utterance, and not just knowledge of its "stimulus meaning".

A quite different, but ultimately also unsuccessful, contrast between fact and interpretation has been defended by Gadamer: statements as to what words mean (e.g., *parlez-vous Français* means "Do you speak French?") are to be classsified as *facts*, while interpretations of, say, religious traditions and of texts within those traditions belong to "hermeneutics". On Gadamer's view, interpreting "Love your neighbor as yourself" breaks up into two parts: saying what the meaning of the sentence is (fact) and *interpreting* that meaning (interpretation or hermeneutics). Thus, while Quine's aim is to separate *scientific* fact (observational data) from even minimal connection with the ascription of linguistic meaning, Gadamer's aim is to separate ascriptions of linguistic meaning from "interpretation" in a more elevated sense. As Gadamer puts it: "To understand a language is not itself any real understanding (*Verstehen*) and includes *no* real interpretation process, but is a life-accomplishment."[12]

What lends Gadamer's view plausibility is that in the case of the languages which most interest him – for example, the languages in which the Bible and most of the commentaries on the Bible have been written – there are long established translations of the words and established ways of translating most sentences. This justifies calling truths about the meanings (translations) of these words and sentences "facts" – and, indeed, they *are* facts, for they function as such. But the case of radical translation is quite different. To know whether *bosorkanyok* means "witch" I must understand a whole culture; and while this is indeed simply a *Lebensvollzug* ("life accomplishment") for someone brought up in the culture, for an outsider it is decidedly an *Interpretationssvorgang* ("interpretation process"). Like Quine, but in a different area, Gadamer fails to see that what he takes to be "fact" is conceptually connected to what he takes to be "interpretation" – indeed, in this case the content of the "fact", if it is one, that *bosorkanyok* means "witch" is given by the explanation of what we are calling "witchcraft" in that culture. The interpretation is not even notionally separable from the fact.

In the second lecture, we saw that there is also a holistic element in the thinking of the later Wittgenstein. For Wittgenstein, as is well known, a language belongs to a "form of life" (in the Lectures on Aesthetics, he speaks of just how much would be required to appreciate African art as a native appreciates it, and how different such appreciation – e.g., the *ability to point out relevant features* – is from the appreciation of the same art by even an informed connoisseur). But a form of life is not factorizable into a set of beliefs about "facts" and a bunch of "values".[13] (In addition, I have had occasion to refer to *On Certainty* in illustrating the interdependence of fact and theory.)

Many years ago, Morton White spoke of a "revolt against formalism" in connection with pragmatism.[14] This revolt against formalism is not a denial of the utility of formal models in certain contexts; but it manifests itself in a sustained critique of the idea that formal models, in particular, systems of symbolic logic, rule books of inductive logic, formalizations of scientific theories, etc. – describe a condition to which rational thought either can or should aspire. Wittgenstein, as you all know, began his career on the formalist side and spent the whole latter part of his life as an antiformalist. Indeed, *On Certainty* explicitly uses images of plasticity and fluidity ("In time, the banks and the river may change places."). We have also seen that, although Richard Rorty describes himself as a "pragmatist" and an admirer of the later Wittgenstein, his habit of dichotomizing human thought into speech within "criterion governed language games" and speech "outside" language games is both unpragmatist and un-Wittgensteinian.

But have we lost the world?

If the features of pragmatism we have been discussing are appealing, they may also seem threatening. As I said in the first lecture, holism may seem to threaten the loss of the world. If fact, value, theory and interpretation interpenetrate in the ways I have described in these lectures, then are we not committed to a "coherence theory of truth"?

Coherence theorists have always pointed out that what they require for truth is not mere coherence of *sentences* but coherence of *beliefs* and that we are not free to *believe* anything we want. Belief is under *causal* constraints. For example, in "A Coherence Theory of Truth and Knowledge",[15] Donald Davidson attempted to convince us that a coherence theory of truth is not so bad, provided we remember that one of the constraints on interpretation is that our words should be interpreted, in most cases, as referring to the sorts of things with which we have had causal (and especially perceptual) interactions. But Davidson's argument does not work for two reasons. The first reason is that if "the cause" is supposed to be something non-conceptual, something simply "built into" the extra-linguistic world, then we get a monstrously unrealistic view of causation.[16] One cannot say, as, for example, Jerry Fodor does, that what makes it the case that the word *cat* refers to cats is that "cats cause cat-tokenings". The question, "What is *the cause* of Jones's using the word cat?" has no meaning at all, apart from a context. *In a* context, depending on the interests of the questioner, the answer may be "The fact that the Anglo-Saxon word was *cat*", "The meow she just heard", etc. Nor, for that matter, can we imagine that the world divides itself into "sorts" in just one determinate way. Davidson avoids these problems by speaking of what the interpretation of our words would be *from the point of view of an omniscient interpreter*. But, and this is the second reason his argument does not work, the very reference to an *interpreter*, omniscient or not, misses the depth of the problem.

Davidson writes as if the only problem were ordinary scepticism, the sort of scepticism that assumes that our utterances *are* true or false, and worries that we cannot *know* which they are.[17] But the real worry is that *sentences cannot be true or false of an external reality if there are no justificatory connections between things we say in language and any aspects of that reality whatsoever*. If that is one's worry – and that is the *deep* worry – then saying "If there *were* an omniscient interpreter, your utterances would be interpreted by that interpreter as having truth conditions which refer to extralinguistic things and events" is no help. It is no help because, if our only model of language is a model of a scheme which is *closed* under justificatory relations, a scheme in which literally *nothing* reaches outside of language (except for the fact that there are brute causal forces acting on language, forces which have no one "built in" description), then we will not be able to see *how there could be speakers or interpreters at all*, and *a fortiori* we will not be able to see how there could be an *omniscient* interpreter. The assumption that the notion of an omniscient interpreter so much as makes sense begs the entire question.

John McDowell has suggested[18] that the solution is to think of perception as an exercise of our conceptual powers, and not merely of our sense organs, so that (contrary to what is said by Davidson and many others) a non-linguistic event, e.g., hearing a cat, can *justify*, and not merely *cause*, a linguistic event ("Mitty wants some food"). This suggestion would probably meet with the approval of William James. But it may also make the problem seem worse rather than better.

An example may help us to see how perception can be an exercise of our conceptual abilities. Suppose I perceive a resistor lying on a table. I know what a resistor is and what a resistor looks like. I am not supposing that I think the words "that is a resistor" (I rarely if ever think the words "that is a chair" when I see a chair), but I would be able to answer the question "what is that thing?". How does my visual experience differ from the visual experience I had when I saw the same thing but did not know what it was?

Well, consider the auditory experience I have when I now hear an English sentence. When I returned to the United States from France at age eight not speaking any English,[19] even a simple English sentence – say, "We're going to eat in a few minutes" sounded like *noise*. Now that sentence *says* something to me; I cannot hear it as noise.[20] I can have a similar experience today: if I learn the meaning of an Italian sentence that I did not previously understand, the way I *hear* that sentence will change. To be sure, I am aware that the sounds did not "change"; but what I hear is not correctly described as the sounds I heard before *plus* an interpretation. Nor is what I see when I see a resistor correctly described as the visual experience I had when the resistor was just a "thing" *plus* an interpretation. As William James put it, the perception is "thought and sensation *fused*". The knowledge that what I am seeing is a resistor and the "sensation" are not two *components* of the experience. The experience is not factorizable, any more than the experience of hearing someone say "We're going to eat in a few minutes" is factorizable into the sound I heard when that was still unintelligible and the knowledge that what is being said is that we are going to eat in a few minutes.

John McDowell's point goes beyond James's phenomenological observation in noting that once we think of hearing and seeing as *accessing information from the environment* – something with full right to be regarded as a rational accomplishment – there is no reason to accept the dictum that a perception can only *cause* (and not *justify*) a verbalized thought. The reason that I said a few moments ago that this may make the threat of loss of the world seem worse rather than better is that if perception is always already informed with conceptual content, that content cannot be thought of as always benign. Our concepts may contaminate our perceptions as well as "inform" them; perceptions supply misinformation as well as information. Here I do not have in mind the relatively harmless possibility (although it was not always thought of as harmless in the history of philosophy!) of illusions of a traditional kind, e.g., mistaking a reflection for a person, or a shadow for an animal. I have in mind seeing someone as a *witch* (as in the persecutions that swept Europe and the American colonies in the late Renaissance), or seeing a person as a representative of an "inferior race". If we can see resistors, we can also see (or think we see) *witches*. It will seem to some that McDowell has not removed the danger of losing the world but rather extended it to perception itself.

The pragmatist response to scepticism

Part of the pragmatist response is the Peircean distinction between real and philosophical doubt that I mentioned in my first lecture. I know that the evils and tragedies that I see around me are not caused by witches; I also know that a few centuries ago intelligent people believed the contrary. That knowledge can, and according to pragmatists *should*, produce a healthy awareness of human fallibility; but it should not, and indeed cannot, produce universal scepticism. One cannot summon up real doubt at will ("Doubting is not as easy as lying", Peirce once said). Ceasing to believe anything at all is not a real human possibility. The fact that we have sometimes been mistaken in even very fundamental beliefs cannot, by itself, make me doubt any *specific* belief. The fact that there are no witches does not make me worry that perhaps there are no resistors.

This too may seem like "small comfort". If the fact that we are sometimes wrong is not a reason for doubting – *really* doubting – any *particular* belief, neither is the Peircean point just reviewed a reason for trusting any particular belief. What we want, it may seem, is a method for telling which of our beliefs are *really* justified, by perception or otherwise, and which are not. But is not the desire for such a method a hankering for an impossible

Archimedean point, a vestige of what Dewey excoriated as "the quest for certainty"?

Yes and No. A "method" in the sense of an algorithm which solves all of our epistemological problems is a philosopher's fantasy (recall what I said about the pragmatist "revolt against formalism"). But, Peirce also reminded us – and this side of pragmatism was continued by John Dewey throughout his long philosophical life – that the fact that we cannot reduce scientific inquiry (in the generous sense of "scientific" that both Peirce and Dewey tried to introduce to us) to an algorithm, on the one hand, nor provide a metaphysical guarantee that any of our beliefs or methods will never need revision, on the other, does not mean that we don't know *anything* about how to conduct inquiry. Peirce and Dewey believed that we *have* learned a good deal about how inquiry should be conducted – learned from our past experience with inquiry – and that some of what we have learned applies to inquiry in general, and not just to particular kinds of inquiry or particular subject matters.

A view like Peirce's or Dewey's will not be intelligible if one starts with what I may call a "Carnapian" view of inquiry. For this reason, we need to recall the differences between the way in which a philosopher like John Dewey sees the scientific method and the way in which a philosopher like Rudolf Carnap did. It is noteworthy that in Carnap's great work on inductive logic[21] – the work to which he devoted almost all of his energy in the last two decades of his life – there is virtually no reference to *experiment*. The word does not even occur as an entry in the index to *The Logical Foundations of Probability*! Scientific theories are confirmed by "evidence", in Carnap's systems of inductive logic, but it is immaterial (that is to say, there is no way to represent the difference in the formalism) whether that evidence – those "observation sentences" – is obtained as the result of intelligently directed experimentation, or it just happens to be available. Passive observation and active intervention are not distinguished, and the question, whether one has actually tried to *falsify* the hypotheses that have been "highly confirmed" is not a question which can be asked or answered *in* the languages Carnap constructed. Even more important, for our purposes, is the fact that the term that Carnap used to characterize his own stance in the *Aufbau*, the term "methodological solipsism", could also be applied, though in a different sense, to this later philosophical work of Carnap's. For just as it makes no difference from the point of view of Carnapian inductive logic whether our observation is passive or active, whether we just look or whether we intervene, it also makes no difference whether observation is *cooperative* or not. Fundamentally, the standpoint is that of a single isolated spectator who makes observations through a one-way mirror and writes down observation sentences. Appraising theories for their cognitive virtues is then simply a matter of using an algorithm to determine whether a sentence has a mathematical relation to another sentence (the conjunction of the observation sentences the observer has written down), on this picture. The scientific method is reconstructed as a method of *computation*, computation of a function like Carnap's famous "c*". [22]

The pragmatist picture is totally different. For Peirce and Dewey, inquiry is cooperative human interaction with an environment; and both aspects, the active intervention, the active manipulation of the environment, and the cooperation with other human beings, are vital. The first aspect, the aspect of intervention, is connected with pragmatist fallibilism. Of course, Carnap was also a fallibilist, in the sense of recognizing that future obser-vation might disconfirm a theory which is today very well confirmed; but for the pragmatists this was not fallibilism enough. Before Karl Popper was even born, Peirce[23] emphasized that very often ideas will not be falsified unless we go out and actively *seek* falsifying experiences. Ideas must be put under strain, if they are to prove their worth; and Dewey and James both followed Peirce in this respect.

For the positivists – e.g., for both Carnap and Reichen-bach – the most primitive form of scientific inquiry, and the form that they studied first when they constructed their (otherwise very different) theories of induction, was induction by simple enumeration. The model is always a single scientist who determines the colors of the balls drawn successively from an urn, and tries to estimate the frequencies with which those colors occur among the balls remaining in the urn. For the pragmatists, the model is a *group* of inquirers trying to produce good ideas and trying to test them to see which ones have value.

In addition, as I already pointed out, the model of an *algorithm*, like a computer program, is rejected. According to the pragmatists, whether the subject be science or ethics, what we have are maxims and not algorithms; and maxims themselves require contextual interpretation. The problem of subjectivity and intersubjectivity was in the minds of the pragmatists from the beginning – not as a metaphysical worry about whether we have access to a world at all, but as a real problem in human life. They insisted[24] that when one human being in isolation tries to interpret even the best maxims for himself and does not allow others to criticize the way in which he or she interprets those maxims, or the way in which he or she applies them, then the kind of "certainty" that results is *in practice* fatally tainted with subjectivity. Even the notion of "truth" makes no sense in such a "moral solitude" for "truth presupposes a standard external to the thinker".[25] Notions like "simplicity", for example, have no clear meaning at all unless inquirers who have proven their competence in the practice of inquiry are able to agree, to some extent at least, on which theories do and which theories do not possess "simplicity". The introduction of new ideas for testing likewise depends on cooperation, for any human being who rejects inputs from other human beings runs out of ideas sooner rather than later, and begins to consider only ideas which in one way or another reflect the prejudices he or she has formed. Cooperation is necessary both for the formation of ideas and for their rational testing.

But that cooperation must be of a certain kind in order to be effective. It must, for example, obey the principles of discourse ethics.[26] Where there is no opportunity to challenge accepted hypotheses by criticizing the evidence upon which their acceptance was based, or the application of the norms of scientific inquiry to that evidence, or by offering rival hypotheses, and where questions and suggestions are systematically ignored, then the scientific enterprise always suffers. When relations among scientists become relations of hierarchy and dependence, or when scientists instrumentalize other scientists, again the scientific enterprise suffers.[27] Dewey was not naive. He was aware that there are power plays in the history of science as there are in the history of every human institution. He would not have been surprised by the findings of historians and sociologists of science; but he differs from some of our contemporary ones in holding that it makes sense to have a *normative* notion of science.

It is not only that, on Dewey's conception, good science

requires respect for autonomy, symmetric reciprocity, and discourse ethics – that could be true even if scientific theories and hypotheses were, in the end, to be tested by the application of an algorithm, such as the inductive logic for which Carnap hoped – but, as we already observed, the very *interpretation* of the *non*-algorithmic standards by which scientific hypotheses are judged depends on cooperation and discussion structured by the same norms. Both for its full development and for its full application to human problems, science requires the *democratization of inquiry.*[28]

What I have just offered is, in part, an *instrumental* justification of the democratization of inquiry. But Dewey opposes the philosophers' habit of dichotomization. In particular, he opposes both the dichotomy "pure science/ applied science" and the dichotomy "instrumental value/ terminal value". Pure science and applied science are interdependent and interpenetrating activities, Dewey argues.[29] And similarly, instrumental values and terminal values are interdependent and interpenetrating. Science helps us to achieve many goals other than the attainment of knowledge for its own sake, and when we allow inquiry to be democratized simply because doing so helps us achieve those practical goals, we are engaged in goal-oriented activity. At the same time, *even when we are engaged in a goal-oriented activity* we also are guided by norms of rationality which have become terminal values for us, and which cannot be separated from the modern conception of "rationality" itself. Moreover, we are not – nor were we ever – interested in knowledge *only* for its practical benefits; curiosity is coeval with the species itself, and pure knowledge is always, to some extent, and in some areas, a terminal value even for the least curious among us. It is not, *for us,* any longer just a sociological-descriptive fact that choosing theories for their predictive power and simplicity, and fostering democratic cooperation and openness to criticism in the generation and evaluation of theories, are part of the nature of scientific inquiry; these norms describe the way we *ought* to function when the aim is knowledge.

Rortian Relativism

Rorty will reply that all of this is excellent advice, but we should not pretend that it rests on anything but the interests and preferences of our "Western democratic culture". Lyotard will worry that even this advice is exploitative – valorizing democratic discussion may oppress the "inarticulate", according to this "postmodern" thinker. But refusal to discuss certainly does not help anyone – even Lyotard does not think we will benefit from mindless activism. And Rorty's constant insistence that talk of "truth" is merely emotive (a "compliment" we pay to certain beliefs) rests on his curious notion that we are connected to the world "causally but not semantically'. Rorty is in the grip of the picture that the Eliminative Materialism is true of the Noumenal World, even if he is debarred by the very logic of his own position from stating that belief. What the pragmatist thinkers I have discussed in these lectures had in common was the conviction that the solution to the problem of "loss of the world" is to be found in action and not in metaphysics (or "postmodern" anti-metaphysics, either). Peirce and James and Dewey would have said that democratically conducted inquiry is to be trusted; not because it is infallible, but because the way in which we will find out where and how our procedures need to be revised is through the process of inquiry itself. (These pragmatists would have added that what we have learned about inquiry in general applies to ethical inquiry in particular.) At the same time, James and Wittgenstein would have asked us to remember that what is publicly verified (or even what is intersubjectively "warrantedly assertable") is not all of what any human being or any culture can live by: James in *The Varieties of Religious Experience* and Wittgenstein in *Lectures and Conversations on Aesthetics, Psychoanalysis, and Religious Belief* and *On Certainty* explore the problems posed by what might be called the limits of intersubjectivity. The need for intersubjectively validated knowledge, the need for tolerance, and the need for forms of life that rest on existential commitments that not everyone can or should make, are all real needs. There is plenty for philosophy to do in exploring those needs; but telling us again and again that 'there is nothing outside the text",[30] or that all our thought is simply "marks and noises" which we are "caused" to produce by a blind material world to which we cannot so much as *refer*,[31] is not an exploration of any of them, but a fruitless oscillation between a linguistic idealism which is largely a fashionable "put on" and a self-refuting scientism. I hope to have made it plausible that there is a better alternative, and to have inspired you to explore that alternative further.

Notes

1 On the impossibility of factoring such a judgment into a "value component" and a "descriptive component" see my *Reason, Truth and History* (Cambridge: Cambridge Univer-

sity Press, 1981), especially Chapter 9, and John McDowell, "Are Moral Requirements Hypothetical Imperatives?", *Proceedings of the Aristotelian Society*, suppl. vol. 52 (1978) and "Virtue and Reason", *Monist* 62 (1979).

2 On this sort of description, see Wittgenstein's discussion of aesthetic appreciation in *Lectures and Conversations on Aesthetics, Psychology and Religious Belief*, edited by Cyril Barrett (Berkeley, Cal.: University of California Press, 1966). Note in particular Wittgenstein's observation that the word *beautiful* "plays an absolutely minor role".

3 For example, although Reichenbach stressed the way in which observations are theory loaded in his 1920 *Relativity Theory and Apriori Knowledge*, his famous "vindication of induction" in *Experience and Prediction* ignores this. Carnap's writing displays a similar oscillation between recognizing the interdependence of observation and theory, most notably in *The Logical Syntax of Language*, and (in his later writing) treating observation statements (which are said to be "completely interpreted") as radically different from theoretical statements (which are said to be only "partially interpreted").

4 Most famously C. S. Peirce. For a synoptic view of Peirce's philosophy see his *Reasoning and the Logic of Things*, ed. Ken Ketner and H. Putnam (Cambridge, Mass.: Harvard University Press, 1992).

5 For example, if I am not in a spaceship in orbit.

6 In conversation, Rogers Albritton has objected to calling such statements as "I see a chair" *theory loaded* on the grounds that these generalizations are not *part of the meaning* of the statement. But Wittgenstein's point was that something may function as a pivot on which the language game turns *even though* "in time the bank and the river may change places" – we do not need *analytic* implications here to see that the "fact" and the "generalizations" depend on one another for their very intelligibility in our language game *as it is right now*.

7 Ian Hacking, *Representing and Intervening* (Cambridge: Cambridge University Press, 1983).

8 *Ibid.*, p. 23.

9 In his *Lectures on the Foundations of Mathematics*, ed. Cora Diamond (Chicago: University of Chicago Press, 1989).

10 In his reply to me in *The Philosophy of W. V. Quine* (LaSalle, Ill.: Open Court, 1986).

11 Note that in present-day European languages, "witch" has *no* 'stimulus meaning" for most speakers, and is thus not an "observation sentence" in Quine's sense, while *bosorkanyok* is, by hypothesis, an observation sentence in the jungle language. But translating *bosorkanyok* as "witch" and *not* as "ugly old woman with a wart on her nose" – even though the latter sentence is an observation sentence, and does have the same stimulus meaning as *bosorkanyok* – may be right!

12 "Eine Sprache verstehen ist selbst noch gar kein wirkliches Verstehen und schliesst *keinen* Interpretationssvorgang ein, sondern ist ein Lebensvollzug," *Wahrheit und Methode* (Tübingen: Mohr Verlag, 1986), p. 388.

13 For a brilliant discussion of this aspect of Wittgenstein's thought, see John McDowell's "Noncognitivism and Rule Following," in S. H. Holtzman and C. M. Leich (eds.), *Wittgenstein: to Follow a Rule* (London and New York: Routledge and Kegan Paul, 1981).

14 Cf. Morton White's *Social Thought in America: The Revolt Against Formalism* (New York, 1949).

15 In E. Lepore (ed.), *Truth and Interpretation: Perspectives on the Philosophy of Donald Davidson* (Oxford: Blackwell, 1984).

16 I do not wish to suggest that this *is* what Donald Davidson thinks, although it *is* what Jerry Fodor thinks (in *Psychosemantics*, for example). On why this is an unrealistic view of causation see my "Is the Causal Structure of the Physical Itself Something Physical?" in *Realism with a Human Face* (Cambridge, Mass.: Harvard University Press, 1990) and

my *Renewing Philosophy* (Cambridge, Mass.: Harvard University Press, 1992).

17 I am indebted to John McDowell's forthcoming *Mind and World* for this observation and for the point which follows, although he should not be held responsible for my formulation.

18 This is the theme of the book cited in the preceding note.

19 I was born in Chicago, but I was taken to France by my father and mother when I was a few months old, and did not learn English until we came back to the States in 1934.

20 According to Jerry Fodor (*The Modularity of Mind*), the reason for this is that a "module" – a subpersonal automatic processor – has been formed in my brain which "recognizes" this sentence using a fairly simple heuristic. Fodor uses this hypothesis to *deny* that the recognition of the sentence is a conceptual activity. But this is a confusion on more than one ground: (1) If the module were removed from my brain and kept alive artificially and stimulated electrically the result would not be an 'auditory sense datum" occurring in a handful of neurons, but just a physical event. By identifying the outputs of his modules with *appearances*, Fodor is making a mistake against which James repeatedly warns in the *Principles of Psychology* [cf. my review of Fodor's book in *Cognition*]: the fact that a bit of machinery in the brain is *necessary* for a mental function does not mean that we can simply *identify* the mental function and the operation of the machinery. Hearing and understanding a sentence involves much *more* than the operation of the module; although the operation of the module is (if Fodor's theory is right) part of what *enables* us to hear and understand the sentence. (2) If the relevant conceptual knowledge were somehow removed from my brain without disturbing the module, I might have a feeling of "recognizing" the sentence, but this would be followed by the disturbing realization that I had no idea what it meant – this would not be an experience of *hearing someone*

say "We're going to eat in a few minutes", or whatever. It is only with the conceptual system in place that the operation of the subpersonal mechanism enables me to hear *that*. As James points out, the localized "brain traces", etc., that neurobiologists loved to identify with mental functions even in his day may do quite different things depending on what is going on in the rest of the brain and body. As McDowell puts it, hearing a sentence or seeing a chair is accessing information from the environment; *this* is the function of perception, and – since it involves the entire *transaction* between the organism and the environment [here I am using John Dewey's way of conceptualizing the situation to explain McDowell's point!] – perception should not be thought of as taking place in the head, even though the neurological mechanisms on which it depends are in the head. *The mind is not in the head.* (3) Another reason Fodor has for wanting speech recognition to be non-conceptual is that on Fodor's theory of meaning (as subsequently developed in *Psychosemantics* and *The Modularity of Mind*), the *meaning* of the words is not determined, even in part, by the conceptual relations among the various notions I have mastered – e.g., between "minute" and my other time concepts – but depends *only* on "nomic relations" between the words (e.g., *minute*) and the corresponding "universals" (e.g., minutehood). These "universals" are just word-shaped objects which Fodor's metaphysics projects out into the world for the words to latch on to via mysterious "nomic relations"; the whole story is nothing but a "naturalistic" version of the Museum Myth of Meaning.

21 R. Carnap, *The Logical Foundations of Probability* (Chicago: University of Chicago Press, 1950), and *The Continuum of Inductive Methods* (Chicago: University of Chicago Press, 1952).

22 Cf. *The Logical Foundations of Probability*, 294 ff.

23 "It is a very grave mistake to attach much importance to

the antecedent likelihood of hypotheses, except in extreme cases; because likelihoods are mostly merely subjective, and have so little real value, that considering the remarkable opportunities that they will cause us to miss, in the long run attention to them does not pay. Every hypothesis should be put to the test by forcing it to make verifiable predictions." *Collected Papers of Charles Saunders Peirce*, volume V. *Pragmatism and Pragmaticism*, ed. C. Hartshorne and P. Weiss (Cambridge, Mass.: Harvard University Press, 1934), p. 419 [5.599].

24 Cf. The omnipresence of this theme in Peirce's philosophy is the subject of K. O. Apel's *C. S. Peirce, from Pragmatism to Pragmaticism* (Amherst, Mass.: University of Massachusetts, 1981). See also James in "The Moral Philosopher and the Moral Life", and Dewey in *Experience and Nature*, Chapter V, "Nature, Communication, and Meaning" (New York: Dover, 1958) – first published in 1925 by Open Court.

25 James in "The Moral Philosopher and the Moral Life".

26 This is the approach to ethics made famous by Habermas, and K. O. Apel. Cf. Habermas' *The Theory of Communicative Action*, in two volumes (Boston: Beacon Press, 1980), and Apel's *Diskurs und Verantwortung: Das Problem des Übergangs zur Postkonventionellen Moral* (Suhrkamp, 1985). For a comparison of discourse ethics and pragmatism see "A Reconsideration of Deweyan Democracy", last chapter of *Renewing Philosophy* (Cambridge, Mass.: Harvard University Press, 1992).

27 I have used the vocabulary of Agnes Heller's *A Philosophy of Morals* (Oxford: Blackwell, 1990) in this sentence to bring out the "ethical" tone of the norms governing scientific inquiry.

28 To the objection that we do not consider *all* views when a scientific hypothesis is under discussion – instructed opinions are the ones that matter – Dewey's reply (in the *Logic*) is that, while this is true, there *is* a stage at which lay

opinion should count. The *application* of science is also a
test of the hypotheses applied, and that test needs to be
under democratic control. (Think of what happens when
medical drugs and devices are tested only by the companies
that manufacture them!)

29 This is discussed in R. A. Putnam's and my "Epistemology
as Hypothesis".
30 This is a famous (and gnomic) saying of Derrida's.
31 This is the way Rorty presented his view at a conference
on Truth in Paris (May 3, 1990) sponsored by the Collège
Internationale de Philosophie.

Bibliography of the Writings of Hilary Putnam

I BOOKS

1964

1 With Paul Benacerraf (Eds.): *Philosophy of Mathematics: Selected Readings*, Second edition, Cambridge University Press, Cambridge/New York, 1983.

1971

2 *Philosophy of Logic*, Harper & Row, New York.

1975

3 *Mathematics, Matter and Method. Philosophical Papers, Volume 1*, Cambridge University Press, Cambridge/New York.
4 *Mind, Language and Reality. Philosophical Papers, Volume II*, Cambridge University Press, Cambridge/New York.

1978

5 *Meaning and the Moral Sciences*, Routledge & Kegan Paul, London.

1981

6 *Reason, Truth and History*, Cambridge University Press, Cambridge/New York.

1983

7 *Realism and Reason, Philosophical Papers, Volume III*, Cambridge University Press, Cambridge/New York.
8 With Carl G. Hempel and Wilhelm K. Essler (Eds.): *Methodology, Epistemology and Philosophy of Science. Essays in Honor of Wolfgang Stegmuller on the Occasion of His 60th Birthday*, D. Reidel, Dordrecht.

1985

9 With Wilhelm Karl Essler and Wolfgang Stegmuller (Eds.): *Epistemology, Methodology and Philosophy of Science. Essays in Honor of Carl G. Hempel on the Occasion of his 80th Birthday*, D. Reidel, Dordrecht.

1987

10 *The Many Faces of Realism*. (The Paul Carus Lectures, Washington 1985), Open Court, La Salle, Ill.

1988

11 *Representation and Reality*, Massachusetts Institute of Technology Press, Cambridge, Mass.

1990

12 *Realism with a Human Face*, edited by James Conant, Harvard University Press, Cambridge, Mass.
13 *The Meaning of the Concept of Probability in Application to Finite Sequences*, PhD Thesis, University of California, Los Angeles 1951. With "Introduction Some Years Later." Garland, New York/London.

1992

14 *Renewing Philosophy* (The Gifford Lectures, St Andrews 1990), Harvard University Press, Cambridge, Mass.
15 With Ted Cohen and Paul Guyer (Eds.): *Pursuits of Reason: Essays Presented to Stanley Cavell*, Texas Technical University Press, Lubbock, Texas.

1994

16 *Words and Life*, edited by James Conant, Harvard University Press, Cambridge, Mass.

II ESSAYS

1954

1 "Synonymity and the Analysis of Belief Sentences," in: *Analysis* **14**, 114–122.

1956

2 "A Definition of Degree of Confirmation for Very Rich Languages," in: *Philosophy of Science* **23**, 58–62.
3 "Mathematics and the Existence of Abstract Entities," in: *Philosophical Studies* **7**, 81–88.
4 "Reds, Greens and Logical Analysis," in: *Philosophical Review* **65**, 206–217.

1957

5 "Arithmetic Models for Consistent Formulae of Quantification Theory," in: *Journal of Symbolic Logic* **22**, 110f.
6 "Decidability and Essential Undecidability," in: *Journal of Symbolic Logic* **22**, 39–54.
7 "Psychological Concepts, Explication and Ordinary Language," in: *The Journal of Philosophy* **54**, 94–99.
8 "Red and Green all Over Again: A Rejoinder to Arthur Pap," in: *Philosophical Review* **66**, 100–103.
9 "Three-Valued Logic," in: *Philosophical Studies* **8**, 73–80.

1958

10 With Martin Davis: "Reductions of Hilbert's Tenth Problem," in: *Journal of Symbolic Logic* **23**, 183–187.

11 With Paul Oppenheim: "Unity of Science as a Working Hypothesis," in: Herbert Feigl/Michael Scriven/Grover Maxwell (Eds.): *Concepts, Memories and the Mind-Body Problem, Minnesota Studies in the Philosophy of Science II,* University of Minnesota Press, Minneapolis, 3–36.

1959

12 "Memo on 'Conventionalism'," *Publication of the Minnesota Center for the Philosophy of Science,* 22 March 1959, University of Minnesota Press, Minneapolis.

1960

13 "An Unsolvable Problem in Number Theory," in: *Journal of Symbolic Logic* **25**, 220–232.
14 "Minds and Machines," in: Sidney Hook (Ed.): *Dimensions of Mind,* State University of New York Press, Albany, NY.
15 With Martin Davis: "A Computing Procedure for Quantification Theory," in: *Journal of the Association for Computing Machines* **7**, 201–215.
16 With Raymond Smullyan: "Exact Separation of Recursively Enumerable Sets Within Theories," in: *Proceedings of the American Mathematical Society* **11**, 575–577.

1961

17 "Comments on the Paper of David Sharp, 'The Einstein–Podolsky–Rosen Paradox Re-Examined'," in: *Philosophy of Science* **28**, 234–239.
18 "Some Issues in the Theory of Grammar," in: The American Mathematical Society, *Proceedings of Symposia in Applied Mathematics* **12**, 25–42.

19 "Uniqueness Ordinals in Higher Constructive Number Classes," in: Yoshua Bar-Hillel (Ed.): *Essays on the Foundations of Mathematics dedicated to A. A. Fraenkel on his 70th Anniversary*, Magnes, Jerusalem, 190–206.

20 With Martin Davis and Julia Robinson: "The Decision Problem for Exponential Diophantine Equations," in: *Annals of Mathematics* **74**, 425–436.

1962

21 "Dreaming and 'Depth Grammar'," in: R. J. Butler (Ed.): *Analytical Philosophy. First Series*, Basil Blackwell, Oxford.

22 "It Ain't Necessarily So," in: *The Journal of Philosophy* **59**, 658–670.

23 "The Analytic and the Synthetic," in: Herbert Feigl and Grover Maxwell (Eds.): *Scientific Explanation. Space and Time. Minnesota Studies in the Philosophy of Science III*, University of Minnesota Press, Minneapolis.

24 "What Theories are Not," in: Ernest Nagel and Patrick Suppes and Alfred Tarski (Eds.): *Logic, Methodology and Philosophy of Science*, Stanford University Press, Stanford, CA.

1963

25 "A Note on Constructible Sets of Integers," in: *Notre Dame Journal of Formal Logic* **4**, 270–273.

26 "An Examination of Grünbaum's Philosophy of Space and Time," in: B. Baumrin (Ed.): *Philosophy of Science: The Delaware Seminar 2. 1962–1963*, Interscience, New York.

27 "Brains and Behaviour," in: R. J. Butler (Ed.): *Analytical Philosophy. Second Series*, Basil Blackwell, Oxford.

28 "'Degree of Confirmation' and Inductive Logic," in: Paul Arthur Schilpp (Ed.): *The Philosophy of Rudolf Carnap*, (The Library of Living Philosophers), Open Court, La Salle, Ill.

29 "Probability and Confirmation," in: *The Voice of America. Forum Philosophy of Science*, US Information Agency.

30 With Martin Davis: "Diophantine Sets Over Polynomial Rings," in: *Illinois Journal of Mathematics* **7**, 251–256.

1964

31 "Discussion: Comments on Comments on Comments: a Reply to Margenau and Wigners," in: *Philosophy of Science* **31/I**, 1–6.

32 "On Families of Sets Represented in Theories," in: *Archiv für mathematische Logik und Grundlagenforschung* **6**, 66–70.

33 'On Hierarchies and Systems of Notations," in: *Proceedings of the American Mathematical Society* **15**, 44–50.

34 "Robots: Machines or Artificially Created Life?," in: *The Journal of Philosophy* **61**, 688–691.

35 With Paul Benacerraf: "Introduction," in: I-1, 1–27.

1965

36 "A Philosopher Looks at Quantum Mechanics," in: Robert G. Colodny (Ed.): *Beyond the Edge of Certainty: Essays in Contemporary Science and Philosophy*, Prentice Hall, Englewood Cliffs, NJ.

37 "Craig's Theorem," in: *The Journal of Philosophy* **62**, 251–259.

38 "How not to Talk About Meaning. Comments on J. J. C. Smart," in: Robert S. Cohen and M. W. Wartowski (Eds.): *Boston Studies in the Philosophy of Science*, Vol. II (In Honor of Philipp Frank), Humanities Press, New York.

39 "Philosophy of Physics," in: Franklin H. Donnell (Ed.): *Aspects of Contemporary American Philosophy*, Physica Verlag, Würzburg.

40 "Trial and Error Predicates and the Solution to a Problem of Mostowski," in: *Journal of Symbolic Logic* 30, 49–57.

41 With Gustav Hensel: "On the Notational Independence of Various Hierarchies of Degrees of Unsolvability," in: *Journal of Symbolic Logic* 30, 69–86.

42 With David Luckham: "On Minimal and Almost Minimal Systems of Notations," in: *Transactions of the American Mathematical Society* 119, 86–100.

43 With Marian Boykan Pour-El: "Recursively Enumerable Classes and their Application to Recursive Sequences of Formal Theories," in: *Archiv für mathematische Logik und Grundlagenforschung* 8, 104–121.

44 With Joseph S. Ullian: "More About 'About'," in: *The Journal of Philosophy* 62, 305–310.

1967

45 "Mathematics Without Foundations," in: *The Journal of Philosophy* 64, 5–22.

46 "Psychological Predicates," in: W. H. Captain and D. D. Merrill (Eds.): *Art, Mind and Religion. Oberlin Colloquium in Philosophy*, University of Pittsburgh Press, Pittsburgh, Pa.

47 "The 'Innateness Hypothesis' and Explanatory Models in Linguistics," in: *Synthese* 17, 12–22.

48 "The Mental Life of Some Machines," in: Henry Castaneda (Ed.): *Intentionality, Minds and Perception*, Wayne State University Press, Detroit, Mich.

49 "The Thesis that Mathematics is Logic," in: Ralph Schoenman (Ed.): *Bertrand Russell. Philosopher of the Century*, Allen & Unwin, London.

50 "Time and Physical Geometry," in: *The Journal of Philosophy* **64**, 240–247.

51 With Burton Dreben: "The Craig Interpolation Lemma," in: *Notre Dame Journal of Formal Logic* **8**, 229–233.

1968

52 "Is Logic Empirical?," in: Robert S. Cohen and M. W. Wartowski (Ed.): *Boston Studies in the Philosophy of Science*, Vol. V, D. Reidel, Dordrecht.

53 With George Boolos: "Degrees of Unsolvability of Constructible Sets of Integers," in: *Journal of Symbolic Logic* **33**, 497–513.

1969

54 "Logical Positivism and the Philosophy of Mind," in: Peter Achinstein and Samuel Barker (Ed.): *The Legacy of Logical Positivism*, Johns Hopkins Press, Baltimore.

55 With Gustav Hensel: "Normal Models and the Field Sigma-star," in: *Fundamenta Mathematicae* **64**, 231–240.

56 With Gustav Hensel and Richard Boyd: "A Recursion-Theoretic Characterization of the Ramified Analytical Hierarchy," in: *Transactions of the American Mathematical Society* **141**, 37–62.

1970

57 "Is Semantics Possible?," in: *Metaphilosophy* **I**, 187–201. Also in: Howard E. Kiefer and Milton K. Munitz (Eds.): *Languages, Belief and Metaphysics*, Vol. I of *Contemporary Philosophic Thought: The International Philosophy Year Conferences at Brockport*, State University of New York Press, Albany, NY.

58 "Liberalism, Radicalism and Contemporary 'Unrest'," in: *Metaphilosophy* 1, 71–74.
59 "On Properties," in: Nicolas Rescher et al. (Eds.): *Essays in Honor of Carl Hempel. A Tribute on the Occasion of his 65th Birthday*, D. Reidel, Dordrecht.
60 With H. B. Enderton: "A Note on the Hyperarithmetical Hierarchy," in: *Journal of Symbolic Logic* 35, 429f.

1971

61 With Stephen Leeds: "An Intrinsic Characterization of the Hierarchy of Constructible Sets of Integers," in: R. O. Grandy and C. E. M. Yates (Eds.): *Logic Colloquium '69*, North-Holland, Amsterdam, 311–350.

1973

62 "Explanation and Reference," in: G. Pearce and P. Maynard (Eds.): *Conceptual Change*, D. Reidel, Dordrecht.
63 "Meaning and Reference," in: *The Journal of Philosophy* 70, 699–711.
64 "Recursive Functions and Hierarchies," in: *American Mathematical Monthly* 80/6, 68–86.
65 "Reductionism and the Nature of Psychology," in: *Cognition* 2, 131–146.
66 With Stephen Leeds: "Solution to a Problem of Grandy's," in *Fundamenta Mathematicae* 81, 99–106.

1974

67 "Comment on Wilfred Sellars," in: *Synthese* 27, 445–455.
68 "Discussion" (on "Scientific Explanation", II-72, with Suppes, Cohen, Achinstein, Braunberger, Shapere,

Hempel, Kuhn, Causey und van Fraassen), in: Frederick Suppes (Ed.): *The Structure of Scientific Theories*, University of Illinois Press, Urbana, Ill., 434–458.

69 "How To Think Quantum-Logically," in: *Synthese* **29**, 55–61.

70 "Philosophy of Language and Philosophy of Science," in: Robert S. Cohen (Ed.): *Boston Studies in the Philosophy of Science* **32**, 603–610.

71 "Reply to Lugg's 'Putnam On Reductionism'," in *Cognition* **3**, 295–298.

72 "Scientific Explanation," in: Frederick Suppe (Ed.): *The Structure of Scientific Theories*, University of Illinois Press, Urbana, Ill., 428–433.

73 "The 'Corroboration' of Theories," in: Paul Arthur Schilpp (Ed.): *The Philosophy of Karl Popper*, Vol. 2, (The Library of Living Philosophers), Open Court, La Salle, Ill.

74 "The Refutation of Conventionalism," in *Nous* **8**, 25–40.

75 With Joan Lukas: "Systems of Notations and the Ramified Analytical Hierarchy," in: *Journal of Symbolic Logic* **39**, 243–253.

1975

76 "Do True Assertions Correspond to Reality?," in: I-4, 70–84.

77 "Introduction: Philosophy of Language and the Rest of Philosophy," in: I-4, VII–XVII.

78 "Introduction: Science as Approximation to Truth," in: I-3, VII–XIV.

79 "Language and Philosophy," in: I-4, 1–32.

80 "Language and Reality," in: I-4, 272–290.

81 'Literature, Science and Reflection," in: *New Literary History* **7**.

82 "Other Minds," in: I-4, 342–361.

83   "Philosophy and Our Mental Life," in: I-4, 291–303.
84   "Reply to Gerald Massey," in I-4, 191–195.
85   "Review of Alfred Ayer: *The Concept of a Person*," in: I-4, 132–138.
86   "The Meaning of 'Meaning'," in: Keith Gunderson (Ed.): *Language, Mind and Knowledge. Minnesota Studies in the Philosophy of Science*, Vol. VII, University of Minnesota Press, Minneapolis.
87   "Truth and Necessity in Mathematics," in: I-3, 1–11.
88   "What is Mathematical Truth?," in: *Historia Mathematica* **2**, 529–543.
89   "What is 'Realism'?," in: *Proceedings of the Aristotelian Society* **76**, 1975–76, 177–194.

1976

90   "Two Dogmas Revisited," in: Gilbert Ryle (Ed.): *Contemporary Aspects of Philosophy*, Oriel Press, London, 202–213.

1977

91   "A Note on 'Progress'," in: *Erkenntnis* **11**, 1–4.
92   "Realism and Reason," in: *Proceedings of the American Philosophical Association* **50**, 483–498.

1978

93   "Meaning and Knowledge" (The John Locke Lectures, Oxford 1976), in: I-5, 7–80.
94   "Meaning, Reference and Stereotypes," in: F. Guenthner and M. Guenthner-Reutter (Eds.): *Meaning and Translation. Philosophical and Linguistics Approaches*, Duckworth, London.

95 "Reference and Understanding," in: I-5, 97–119.

96 "The Philosophy of Science. An Interview," in: Bryan Magee (Ed.): *Men of Ideas. Some Creators of Contemporary Philosophy*, British Broadcasting Corporation, London, 222–239.

97 "There Is at Least One 'A Priori' Truth," in: *Erkenntnis* **13**, 153–170.

98 With Michael Friedman: "Quantum Logic, Conditional Probability and Interference," in: *Dialectica* **32**, 305–315.

1979

99 "Analyticity and Apriority: Beyond Wittgenstein and Quine," in: Peter French (Ed.): *Midwest Studies in Philosophy* **4**, 423–411.

100 "Comment on: 'Empirical Realism and Other Minds'," in: *Philosophical Investigations* **2**, 71f.

101 "Philosophy of Mathematics: A Report," in: Peter D. Asquith and Henry E. Kyburg (Eds.): *Current Research in Philosophy of Science*, Edwards, Ann Arbor, Mich., 368–398.

102 "Reflections on Goodman's *Ways of Worldmaking*," in: *The Journal of Philosophy* **76**, 603–618.

103 "Reply to Dummett's Comments," in: *Avishai Margalit* (Ed.): *Meaning and Use*, D. Reidel, Dordrecht, 226–228.

104 "The Place of Facts in a World of Values," in: Douglas Huff and Omer Prewett (Eds.): *The Nature of the Physical Universe. 1976 Nobel Conference*, John Wiley, New York.

1980

105 "Comments on Chomsky's and Fodor's Replies," in: Massimo Piatelli-Palmarini (Ed.): *Language and Learning. The Debate between Jean Piaget and Noam Chomsky*, Methuen, London, 335–340.

106 "Equivalenza," in: *Enciclopedia Einaudi*, Vol. V, Giulio Einaudi, Turin, 547–564.

107 "How to be an Internal Realist and a Transcendental Idealist (at the Same Time)," in: Rudolf Haller and Walter Grassl (Eds.): *Sprache, Logik und Philosophie. Akten des 4. Internationalen Wittgenstein-Symposiums 1979.* Holder-Pichler-Tempski, Vienna, 100–108.

108 "Models and Reality," in: *Journal of Symbolic Logic* XLV, 464–482.

109 "Possibilità/Necessità," in: *Enciclopedia Einaudi*, Vol. X, Giulio Einaudi, Turin, 976–995.

110 "Referenza/Verità," in: *Enciclopedia Einaudi*. Vol. XI, Giulio Einaudi, Turin, 725–741.

111 "'Si Dieu est mort, alors tout est permis' . . . (réflexions sur la philosophie du langage)," in: *Critique* 36, 791–801.

112 "What is Innate and Why," in: Massimo Piatelli-Palmarini (Ed.): *Language and Learning. The Debate between Jean Piaget and Noam Chomsky*, Methuen, London, 387–409.

1981

113 "Answer to a Question from Nancy Cartwright," in: *Erkenntnis* 16, 407–410.

114 "Convention: A Theme in Philosophy," in: *New Literary History* 13/1.

115 "Philosophers and Human Understanding," in: A. F. Heath (Ed.): *Scientific Explanation. Papers Based on Herbert Spencer Lectures Given in the University of Oxford*, Oxford University Press, Oxford.

116 "Quantum Mechanics and the Observer," in: *Erkenntnis* 16, 193–219.

117 "The Impact of Science on Modern Conceptions of Rationality," in: *Synthese* 46, 359–382.

1982

118 Beyond the Fact/Value Dichotomy," in: *Critica* **14**, 3–12.
119 "Comment on J. A. Fodor's 'Cognitive Science and the Twin Earth Problem'," in: *Notre Dame Journal of Formal Logic* **23**, 98–118.
120 "Pierce the Logician," in: *Historia Mathematica* **9**, 290–301.
121 "Reply to Two Realists," in: *The Journal of Philosophy* **79** (A Symposium on *Reason, Truth and History*), 575–577.
122 "Semantical Rules and Misinterpretations: A Reply to R. M. Martin's 'A Memo on Method'," in: *Philosophy and Phenomenological Research* **42**, 604–609.
123 "Three Kinds of Scientific Realism," in: *The Philosophical Quarterly* **32**, 195–200.
124 "Why Reason Can't Be Naturalized," in: *Synthese* **52**, 3–24.
125 "Why There Isn't a Ready-Made World," in: *Synthese* **51**, 141–168.

1983

126 "Beyond Historicism," in: I-7, 287–303.
127 "Equivalence," in: I-7, 26–45.
128 "Explanation and Reduction," in: *Iyyun* **32**, 123–137.
129 "Introduction: An Overview of the Problem," in: I-7, vii–xviii.
130 "Is there a Fact of the Matter about Fiction?," in: *Poetics Today* **4**, 77–81.
131 "Nelson Goodman's *Fact, Fiction and Forecast*, in: I-12, 303–308.
132 "On Truth," in: Leigh S. Cauman et al. (Eds.): *How Many Questions: Essays in Honor of Sidney Morgenbesser*, Hackett, Indianapolis, 35–36.

133 "Possibility and Necessity," in: I-7, 46–68.
134 "Reference and Truth," in: I-7, 69–86.
135 "Taking Rules Seriously (A Response to M. Nussbaum)," in: *New Literary History* 15, 77–81.
136 "Vagueness and Alternative Logic," in: I-8, 297–314.
137 With Paul Benacerraf: "Introduction," in: I-1, 1–37.

1984

138 "After Ayer, After Empiricism (a Discussion of Ayer's *Philosophy in the Twentieth Century*)," in: *Partisan Review* 5, 265–275.
139 "Is the Causal Structure of the Physical itself Something Physical?," in: Peter A. French and Theodore E. Uehling and Howard K. Wettstein (Eds.): *Midwest Studies in Philosophy* 9 (Causation and Causal Theories), 3–16.
140 "Necessità (A. Ayer)," in: Massimo Piatelli-Palmarini (Ed.): *Livelli da realtà*, Fetrinelli, Mailand.
141 "Proof and Experience," in: *Proceedings of the American Philosophical Society* 128, 31–54.
142 "The Craving for Objectivity," in: *New Literary History* 15, 229–240.

1985

143 "A Comparison of Something with Something Else," in: *New Literary History* 17, 61–79.
144 "A Quick Read is a Wrong Wright," in: *Analysis* 45, 203.
145 "After Empiricism," in: John Rajchman and Cornel West (Eds.): *Post-Analytic Philosophy*, Columbia University Press, New York, 20–30.
146 "Computational Psychology and Interpretation Theory," in: Bruce Vermazen and Merryl Hintikka (Eds.): *Essays*

on Davidson: Actions and Events, Oxford University Press, Oxford.

147 "Reflexive Reflections," in: I-9, 143–154.

1986

148 "Discussion with Paul Churchland about Meaning," in: Zenon Pylyshyn and William Demopoulos" (Eds.): *Meaning and Cognitive Structure. Issues in the Computational Theory of Mind*, Ablex, Norwood, NJ.

149 "Information and the Mental," in: Ernest Lepore and James Leplin (Eds.): *Truth and Interpretation. Perspectives on the Philosophy of Donald Davidson*, Basil Blackwell, Oxford.

150 "Meaning and Our Mental Life," in: Edna Ullman-Margalit (Eds.): *The Kaleidoscope of Science*, D. Reidel, Dordrecht, 17–32.

151 "Meaning Holism," in: Lewis Hahn and Paul Arthur Schilpp (Eds.): *The Philosophy of W. V. O. Quine*, (Library of Living Philosophers), Open Court, La Salle, Ill., 405–431.

152 "Pourquoi les Philosophes?," with Jacques Riche, in: André Jacob (Ed.): *L'Encyclopédie Philosophique Universelle*, Presses Universitaires de France, Paris.

153 "Rationality in Decision Theory and in Ethics," in: *Critica* **18**, 3–16.

154 "The Diversity of the Sciences," in: Philipp Pettit (Ed.): *Metaphysics and Morality. Essays in Honour of J. C. C. Smart*, Basil Blackwell, Oxford, 137–153.

155 "The Realist Picture and the Idealist Picture," in: Venant Cauchy (Ed.): *Philosophie et Culture. Actes du XVIIe Congrès Mondial de Philosophie, 12 August 1983*, Edition Montmorency, Montréal, Vol. 1, 205–211.

1987

156 "Equality and Our Moral Image of the World," in: I-10, 41–62.
157 "Is There Still Anything to Say about Reality and Truth?," in: I-10, 3–22.
158 "Realism and Reasonableness," in: I-10, 23–40.
159 "Reasonableness as a Fact and a Value," in: I-10, 63–86.
160 "Scientific Liberty and Scientific License," in: *Grazer Philosophische Studien* 13, 43–51.
161 "Truth and Convention: On Davidson's Refutation of Conceptual Relativism," in: *Dialectica* 41, 69–77.

1988

162 "After Metaphysics, What?," in: Dieter Henrich and Rolf-Peter Horstmann (Eds.): *Metaphysik nach Kant?* (Stuttgarter Hegel-Kongress 1987, Veröffentlichungen der Internationalen Hegel-Vereinigung, Vol. 17), Klett-Cotta, Stuttgart, 457–466.
163 "Foreword," in: Norman Daniels: *Thomas Reid's "Inquiry": The Geometry of Visibles and the Case for Realism*, Burt Franklin, New York.
164 "La objetividad y la distinción ciencia etica," in: *Dianoia*, 7–25.
165 "Much Ado about Not Very Much (Artificial Intelligence)," in: *Daedalus* 117, 269–282.
166 "Misling," Review of W. V. Quine, *Quiddities* and C. Hookway, *Quine*, in: *The London Review of Books* 10/8, 11–13.

1989

167 An Interview with Professor Hilary Putnam, in: *Cognito* **3**, 85–91.

168 "Model Theory and the 'Factuality' of Semantics," in: Alex George (Ed.): *Reflections on Chomsky*, Basil Blackwell, Oxford, 213–232.

169 "Why is a Philosopher?," in: Avner Cohen and Marcello Dascal (Eds.): *The Institution of Philosophy. A Discipline in Crisis*, Open Court, La Salle, Ill., 61–76.

170 With Ruth Anna Putnam: 'William James's Ideas," in: *Raritan* **8**, 27–44.

171 "A Defense of Internal Realism," in: I-12, 30–42.

172 "A Reconsideration of Deweyan Democracy" (with "Afterword"), in: *Southern California Law Review* **63**, 1671–1697.

173 "An Introduction to Cavell," in: I-15.

174 "How Not to Solve Ethical Problems," in: I-12, 179–192.

175 "Introduction Some Years Later," in: I-13, i–xii.

176 "Is Water Necessarily H$_2$O?," in: I-12, 54–79.

177 "James's Theory of Perception," in: I-12, 54–79.

178 "Objectivity and the Science/Ethics Distinction," in: I-12, 163–178.

179 "Realism with a Human Face," in: I-12, 3–29.

180 "The Idea of Science," in: *Midwest Studies in Philosophy* **16** (The Philosophy of the Human Sciences), 57–64.

181 "The Way the World Is," in: I-12, 261–267.

182 With Ruth Anna Putnam: "Dewey's Logic: Epistemology as Hypothesis," in: *Transactions of the Charles S. Peirce Society* **26**, 407–434.

1991

183 "Does the Disquotational Theory Really Solve All Philosophical Problems?," in: *Metaphilosophy* **22**, 1–13.

184 "Introduction," in: Hans Reichenbach: *The Direction of Time*, ed. by Maria Reichenbach, Texas Technical University Press, Lubbock, Tex.

185 "Logical Positivism and Intentionality," in: A. Philips Griffiths (Ed.): *A. J. Ayer Memorial Essays*, Cambridge University Press, Cambridge (A Supplement to *Philosophy* **30**), 105–116.

186 "Philosophical Reminiscences with Reflections on Firth's Work," in: *Philosophy and Phenomenological Research* **51**, 143–147.

187 "Reichenbach's Metaphysical Picture," in: Wolfgang Spohn (Ed.): *Erkenntnis Orientated. A Centennial Volume for Rudolf Carnap and Hans Reichenbach*, Kluwer, Dordrecht, 61–75.

188 "Replies and Comments," in: *Erkenntnis* **34** (Special Issue on Putnam's Philosophy), 401–424.

189 "Wittgenstein on Religious Belief," in Leroy Rouner (Ed.): *On Community*, University of Notre Dame Press, Notre Dame, Ind.

1992

190 "Can Ethics be Ahistorical?" The French Revolution and the Holocaust," in: Eliot Deutsch (Ed.): *Culture and Modernity: The Authority of the Past. East-West Philosophical Perspectives*, (Proceedings of the Sixth East-West Philosopher's Conference), University of Hawaii Press, Honolulu, Hawaii.

191 "Pope's Essay on Man and Those 'Happy Pieties'," in: I-5.

192 "Replies and Comments," in: *Philosophical Topics* **20** (The Philosophy of Hilary Putnam).

1993

193 "Aristotle after Wittgenstein," in: Robert W. Shaples (Ed.): *Modern Thinkers and Ancient Thinkers* (The Keeling Colloquia at University College, London), UCL Press, London.

194 "On the Slogan 'Epistemology Naturalized'," in: Paulo Leonardi and Marco Santambroggio (Eds.): *On Quine*, Cambridge University Press, Cambridge, forthcoming.

195 "Realism Without Absolutes," in: *The International Journal of Philosophical Studies* 1/2.

196 "Introduction," in: Charles S. Peirce: *Reasoning and the Logic of Things*, ed. by Kenneth L. Ketner, Harvard University Press, Cambridge, Mass.

1994

197 "Pragmatism, Moral Objectivity and Development," in: Jonathan Glover and Martha Nussbaum (Ed.): *Human Capabilities: Women, Men and Equality*, Oxford University Press, Oxford.

198 "The Question of Realism," in: I-16.

199 "To Functionalism and Back Again," in: Samuel Guttenplan (Ed.): *The Blackwell Companion to Philosophy of Mind*, Basil Blackwell, Oxford.

200 "Comments and Replies," in: Peter Clark and Bob Hale (Eds.): *Reading Putnam*, Basil Blackwell, Oxford.

Index

63–4, 75, 76n, 77n; on
aesthetics, 75n; and
criteria, 32–8, 46–9;
ethical purpose in writing,
40, 45–52; on "hinge
propositions", 58; 'holism'
of, 63–64; language *not*
simply rule-following,
35–6; later philosophy of,
45–52n; not an "end of
philosophy" philosopher,
31, 38–41, 52n;
positivistic interpretation
of, 44–8; and "primitive"

societies, 37–38, 50;
refuses to put forward
"theses", 27–28, 31–41;
relation to Kant, 27–45;
Rorty's interpretation of,
32–51; rules not
foundation of language,
35; and the *Tractatus*, 40,
56n; and value, 41;
Winch's interpretation of,
46; Wittgenstein attitude
to religious language, 50;
Wittgenstein's "tone",
39–41

CPSIA information can be obtained
at www.ICGtesting.com
Printed in the USA
BVHW07s0226250718
522554BV00003B/214/P

9 780631 193432